I0517619

THE SERIAL KILLER
TRAVEL GUIDE ACROSS AMERICA

YOUR COAST-TO-COAST
TOUR OF TERROR

JOHNNY TREVISANI
WITH BRIAN WHITNEY

WILD BLUE
PRESS

WildBluePress.com

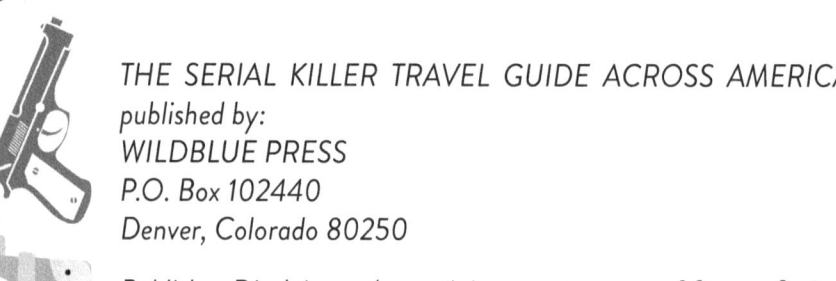

THE SERIAL KILLER TRAVEL GUIDE ACROSS AMERICA
published by:
WILDBLUE PRESS
P.O. Box 102440
Denver, Colorado 80250

Publisher Disclaimer: Any opinions, statements of fact or fiction, descriptions, dialogue, and citations found in this book were provided by the author, and are solely those of the author. The publisher makes no claim as to their veracity or accuracy, and assumes no liability for the content.

WILDBLUE PRESS is registered at the U.S. Patent and Trademark Offices.

ISBN 978-1-964730-63-9 Hardcover
ISBN 978-1-964730-64-6 Trade Paperback
ISBN 978-1-964730-62-2 eBook

Cover design © 2025 WildBlue Press. All rights reserved.

Interior Formatting and Book Cover Design by Elijah Toten
www.totencreative.com

THE SERIAL KILLER
TRAVEL GUIDE ACROSS AMERICA

CONTENTS

YOUR COAST-TO-COAST TOUR OF TERROR

The Serial Killer Travel Guide Across America is not your grandma's travel guide—unless, of course, your grandma had a basement full of teeth.

You won't find charming bed & breakfasts in these pages. No quaint lighthouses or artisanal cheese tours. This is a blood-slicked map of the American psyche, where the interstates stitch together a quilt of horror, each patch soaked in different shades of crimson. A state-by-state descent into the mythos of monsters who walked among us—shopping at the same Safeways, pumping gas at the same Texacos, smiling through the same PTA meetings.

From the moss-drenched killing fields of Texas to the antiseptic apartment horrors of Milwaukee, each chapter is a postcard from Hell: Bundy's Pacific Northwest playground. Gacy's suburban slaughterhouse in Chicagoland. Berkowitz serenading Satan through the back alleys of the Bronx.

It's all here—like a roadside attraction designed by Edgar Allan Poe on a meth binge.

Let this guide be your roadmap through the underbelly of the American Dream. A dream where the picket fences hide crawlspaces and the neighbors never hear the screams because they're too busy watering the lawn.

Buckle up. Keep your windows rolled up and your empathy on ice. We're going deep into the heart of darkness—and not bringing a return ticket.

God bless America. She needs it.

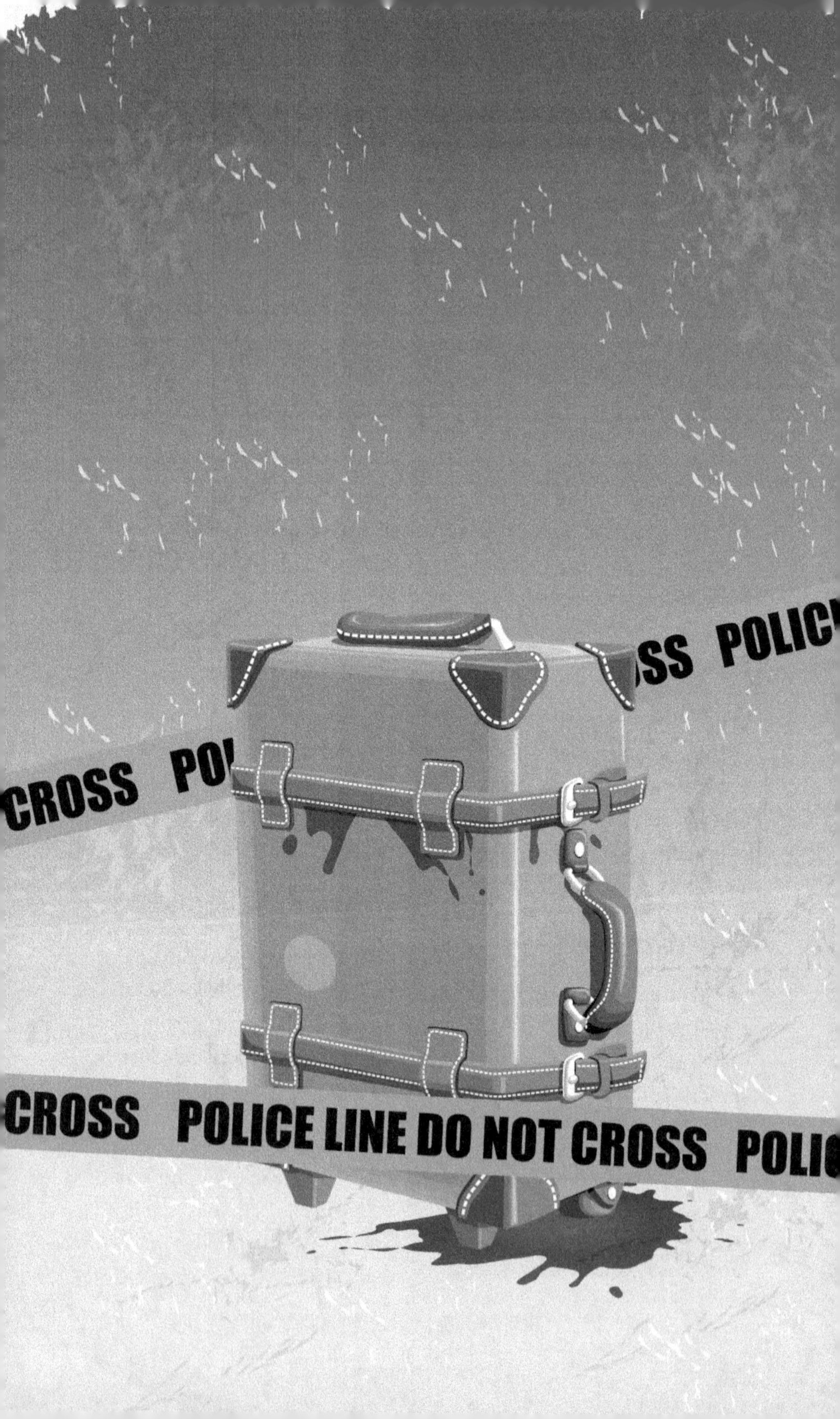
SS POLIC
CROSS PO
CROSS POLICE LINE DO NOT CROSS POLI

NEW ENGLAND

Let's begin our tour in New England.

The saying around these parts is, "Welcome to New England, now please go home." But many who come here never leave, some not by choice.

New England is one of the most fabulous areas to visit in the country. Every year, rich folk "from away" swarm this area to see beautiful fall foliage, stunning rocky coastlines, sandy beaches, and picturesque harbor towns, especially along Cape Cod and the Maine coast. Charming villages with white clapboard houses, covered bridges, and traditional New England architecture abound. If the ocean isn't your jam, perhaps you might enjoy skiing or whitewater rafting in the mountains of Vermont and New Hampshire.

In New England, the word "wicked" means "cool," but there's nothing cool about all the atrocities that have occurred in this region.

The states of New England don't have everything in common, but they coexist, nonetheless.

Maine is like that quiet and introspective friend of yours who likes to hike and is deeply connected to nature. Sure, he's a bit of a loner, a bit of a boozebag, and is suspicious of people from away, but once you get to know him, he'll help you hide the body. He doesn't give two fucks about shoveling a foot of snow but doesn't go to the beach in the summer because it's too crowded.

Massachusetts is like that father you never had: intelligent, educated, wealthy, and influential. That is, until he drinks, then he gets violent as all get out and urinates on himself, just a little.

Vermont is that dude with a trust fund who skis all day and says things like "it's all good" while making maple syrup and voting for Bernie. He does everything right but you hate him anyway.

New Hampshire is like your uncle who shows up on the Fourth of July with a bunch of cheap booze and fireworks he'll eventually shoot at the police when they arrive. No need to raise cash to bail him out—he's got seventy-three thousand dollars in his closet.

Rhode Island is known for goat milk, rich Boston suburbanites, gangs, and beach bums. Wait, who am I kidding? Rhode Island isn't known for anything.

Finally, we have Connecticut. Half the people in Connecticut prefer the Yankees to the Red Sox, so how could they possibly count as New Englanders? Simply put, fuck them.

While New England days are the best, the evenings are when it's time to cozy up by the fire. One fall night, you might look out your window into the calm night. Maple trees line the streets, their branches reaching across the road like gnarled fingers. Most of their leaves have fallen, creating thick drifts that skitter across the brick pavement in the growing darkness. You hear a sound: were those the floorboards creaking behind you?

Probably just a trick of the wind.

PORTLAND, MAINE

John Joubert
Kills: 3+
Span of Activity: August 1982 to
December 1983

Fun Fact:
Joubert was an
Eagle Scout

Ahh, Portland, Maine. Once thought of as a rough-and-tumble city filled with dive bars and cheap eats, this coastal city is now a mecca of tourism filled with expensive condos bought up by out-of-staters named Thad. Still, its brick architecture, cobblestone streets, and proximity to beaches and islands make it a place not to be missed. If one talks to the locals, be prepared to hear, "It's not the same around here." Many miss the days of openly drinking and smoking weed on the wharf, chasing away rats instead of tourists.

While many think of Maine as the land of moose, LL Bean, and rocky coastlines, Portland is more a place for fine dining, craft beer, and finding the occasional dirty needle on the ground. Just know that when you go looking for a lobster roll, don't ask a local where to get one because they pretty much only eat lobster when their cousin Ricky has a couple extra off the boat.

John Joubert grew up with his mother and sister in a run-down apartment in a bad part of Portland, Maine. Joubert didn't have an easy childhood; he was dirt poor, and his mother was controlling and manipulative.

Still, many who have difficult upbringings don't wind up as murderous psychopaths. Which is what Joubert was.

At thirteen years old, he started showing his true self to the world and it wasn't good. Apparently, young John had some

issues. One day, he stabbed a girl with a pencil; the very next day, he rode his bike past a girl and slashed her with a razor blade.

A few years later, he upped his game a bit.

In 1982, when he was twenty-one years old, he attacked eleven-year-old Ricky Stetson, who was out jogging around the Back Cove Trail. His body was found the next day, next to Interstate 295. Stetson was stabbed and strangled. Prominent bite marks were left on his body. This caused one Hell of an uproar with the locals. Things like this simply didn't happen in Maine. In fact, they still don't. Joubert was thankfully one of a kind.

A Portland man was arrested for the murder, which definitely must have sucked. Eighteen months later, the man was released from jail as his teeth didn't match the bite marks on Stetson's body.

The next year, in Nebraska, a thirteen-year-old boy vanished while delivering newspapers. Three days later, his body was found. The boy had been stabbed nine times, tortured, and sexually assaulted.

After a few quiet months, another boy disappeared in Nebraska. Joubert had approached the boy, showed him a knife, and ordered him into his car, where he stabbed him to death.

Then Joubert thankfully messed up. A woman saw a man driving around the area where the boys had gone missing. Suspicious, she began to write down his license plate when the man got out of the car and threatened her. Because that's what you do when you've just killed a couple of young boys and aren't suspected of it. You threaten strangers.

Upon investigation, it turned out the car was driven by John Joubert, who was stationed at a nearby Air Force base. Investigators believed he joined the Air Force to get away from Maine after the murder. A rope consistent with what was used to bind his victims was found in his room.

He was convicted of murder and sentenced to death.

Before his execution, Joubert said, "I just want to say that again I am sorry for what I have done. I do not know if my death will change anything or if it will bring anyone peace. And I just ask the families of Danny Eberle and Christopher Walden and Richard Stetson to please try to find some peace and ask the people of Nebraska to forgive me. That's all."

Asking the families of your victims to find peace. What a lovely sentiment.

On your way out of Portland, check out Holy Donut, which began out of the desire to make a "magical donut made with wholesome, trusted ingredients" and has become one of Portland's biggest tourist traps. These donuts are highly coveted by tourists in the summer, who will often wait in line for close to an hour while being openly mocked by locals, to get a box of donuts made from potatoes.

NORTH BERWICK, MAINE

Richard Steeves
Kills: 6
Span of Activity: June 1965 to
April 1985

Fun Fact: Steeves teaches piano to inmates while incarcerated in the Maine State Prison

Forty miles south of Portland is North Berwick, a lovely town located at Maine's border with New Hampshire. This means it's not close to the ocean, the woods, or the mountains, but it *is* close to two McDonalds and a few Asian massage parlors. North Berwick sits firmly at the intersection of the worst parts of suburban and rural life. It is known for its relaxed pace, mostly because nothing is going on here whatsoever.

Before the first European settlement in 1631, the area was inhabited by Native Americans.

In 1965, it was briefly inhabited by Richard Steeves.

Steeves was born in Waterville, Maine. When he was five years old, his father killed himself. Shortly afterward, his mother gave Richard up to the state, leaving him to be raised in an orphanage. Steeves claimed he was sexually abused as a child. Considering all the terrible things he did as an adult, I tend to believe him. He dropped out of school in his early teens and began racking up minor criminal charges, a trait he continued as an adult. Steeves has been constantly in and out of jail; he has only been a free man for about eighteen months since he was twelve. Which, looking back on it, was eighteen months too long.

In 1965, Steeves killed eighty-three-year-old Harry Staples in North Berwick at his home by beating him with his own cane. A few months later, he broke into the home of a seventy-

year-old man in Rochester, New Hampshire, and stabbed him to death. Two months later, on August 14, he returned to Augusta, Maine, where he broke into the cabin of seventy-three-year-old Lorenzo D. Troyer and brutally beat him to death with a blunt object.

In January 1966, Steeves drove to Ohio. Ostensibly, his car broke down, and he was invited back to the home of two kind strangers who'd stopped to help him out: eighty-four-year-old Lewis Gephart and his thirty-five-year-old son, Francis.

If there's one thing you might have figured out at this point, if you're an old man, you want to stay far away from Steeves. Killing old men was this dude's entire vibe. He bludgeoned both father and son to death, stole the son's car, and drove back to New Hampshire.

When the car was found in New Hampshire with Steeves behind the wheel, he was charged with their murders, making Steeves yet another moron who was busted for murder because he was driving his victim's car.

Steeves pleaded not guilty by reason of insanity. That worked out fabulously for him as the New Hampshire Supreme Court stopped his trial and sent Steeves to the Concord Mental Hospital.

It didn't work out so fabulously for sixty-nine-year-old Bailey Wells. Steeves was released from the mental hospital in 1980, as psychiatrists stated that he was no longer a threat to society.

Spoiler: he was.

A few years later, Steeves broke into Wells' home and killed him. Steeves was found guilty of murder and sentenced to life imprisonment.

He now claims he has been rehabilitated and is seeking parole, but you know the whole "fool me once, shame on you; fool me twice, shame on me" vibe applies here.

He remains imprisoned at Maine State Prison.

Before you leave the area, check out Bentley's Saloon in Arundel. It's a biker bar, which in the old days meant it was kind of a scary place. These days, it means a bunch of overweight old folks with bad ink dancing around to bad cover bands performing "Radar Love."

ALLENSTOWN, NEW HAMPSHIRE

Terry Rasmussen—aka the
Chameleon Killer
Kills: 5+
Span of Activity: November 1978
to June 2002

Fun Fact: Rasmussen lived in several states, including Arizona, Colorado, California, Idaho, Virginia, Texas, Ohio, Oregon, and Hawaii

About an hour west of North Berwick is Allenstown, New Hampshire. Allenstown has been kicking around a long time; it became an official town in 1721. The town is mostly known for Bear Brook State Park. It is a lovely place for hiking if you don't mind hearing numerous gunshots close by while doing so.

New Hampshire has long been known for its rugged individualism (which can be kind of freaky if you ain't expecting it), and Allenstown is no different. The state's motto is *Live Free or Die*. In Southern New Hampshire, this means you're free to work in Boston as a corporate attorney and have a low cost of living. In Northern New Hampshire, this means you're free to wave your gun at strangers and believe in aliens.

Terry Rasmussen took the "or Die" part of the equation to heart.

Rasmussen was born in Denver, Colorado. He enlisted in the United States Navy in 1961 and was discharged in 1967.

Rasmussen married in 1968 and had four children. It didn't go all that well. He was severely abusive, going so far as burning his kids with cigarette butts. His wife left him and took the children after he was arrested for aggravated assault.

This was undoubtedly a good move on her part.

Rasmussen settled in New Hampshire sometime in the late 1970s. He lived in Manchester, going by the name "Bob Evans." Rasmussen was known as the Chameleon Killer because of how many aliases he used over the years. Apparently the "I'm a Complete Asshole Killer" was already taken.

In 1978, Rasmussen began to date Marlyse Honeychurch. A few years later, Bob Evans started to get in a bit of trouble. He was arrested in 1980 for writing bad checks and theft.

Honeychurch got in an argument with her family. To teach them all a lesson about how much she knew what she was doing, she and her two young daughters took off with Rasmussen. Her family never saw them again.

Still using the pseudonym Bob Evans, Rasmussen then began to date a woman named Denise Beaudin. She and her infant daughter left Manchester with Rasmussen in 1981. Authorities believe that Rasmussen killed Beaudin, but her body has never been found.

This creepshow kept the little girl around. Throughout the early 1980s, Rasmussen posed as the little girl's father. He was arrested in 1985 while using the moniker "Curtis Kimball" for driving under the influence and endangering the welfare of a child. Surprisingly, "Curtis Kimball" didn't show up for court. Rasmussen eventually abandoned Beaudin's daughter at an RV park in California.

The bodies of Honeychurch and her children were later found at the bottom of two barrels in Bear Brook State Park. The four died of blunt force trauma to their heads.

In 1999, Rasmussen was going by the name "Larry Vanner" when he met Eunsoon Jun in California. They were married in 2001. This was not a wise decision on Jun's part. She also vanished; later, her body was found buried in cat litter in a crawl space in her home. Rasmussen was arrested and pleaded no contest. He was sentenced to fifteen years to life in prison. He died at age sixty-seven of lung cancer while incarcerated, mostly forgotten by the outside world.

Before you leave Allenstown, check out Bear Brook State Park; with over 10,000 acres, it's the largest state park in the great state of New Hampshire. If you see a bunch of weird-looking men carrying rifles while in the park, don't worry. They're just training.

ESSEX, VERMONT

Israel Keyes
Kills: 11+
Span of Activity: 2001 to February 2012

A few hours northwest of Allenstown is Essex, Vermont. The town was incorporated on June 7, 1763, named after the Earl of Essex. It's a charming town with a mix of entertainment, shopping, and outdoor activities. In Vermont, one can drive an hour in one direction to visit high-end ski resorts and craft breweries where the only locals you'll find are doing dishes in the back; or drive an hour in the other direction to see no one at all. In Vermont, it takes three people to change a lightbulb— one guy changes it and the other two talk about how much new lightbulbs suck.

Vermont has long been known as a haven for those who dig nature and community. It's laid back to the point of ridiculous and has probably the highest ratio of "men with mustaches who wear flannel" in the world. Vermont is where you still see smiling hippies, where residents pride themselves on being able to spot outsiders a mile away.

Israel Keyes was hard to spot.

Keyes was born in Richmond, Utah, in 1978. He was raised in a Mormon family and was homeschooled. He served in the US Army from 1998 through 2000.

A homeschooled Mormon who was in the military. How adorable. What could go wrong?

Keyes was a monster. He began to kill in Washington State in the '90s and confessed to at least one murder in New York State. Keyes also confessed to committing bank robberies in New York and Texas. How's a man supposed to eat when he's driving around the country slaughtering people, after all?

Keyes killed all over the country, but in June 2011, he was in Essex, Vermont. On the night of June 8, Keyes broke into the home of Bill and Lorraine Currier, tied them up, and brought them to an abandoned farmhouse. He then shot and killed Bill Currier before raping and strangling Lorraine to death.

Keyes was in Vermont to kidnap and murder at random. Well, his plan wasn't random, but his victims were. Two years prior to the Curriers' deaths, Keyes hid what he called a "murder kit" in a waterproof bucket near their home, which included a gun, ammunition, and a silencer.

Unlike most serial killers, Keyes didn't have a victim profile. He just liked to kill, and unfortunately for the world, he was good at it. When he went on one of his "murder trips," he always killed far from home and never went back to the same area. He kept his phone turned off, paid cash for everything, and had no connection to his victims. When it came to the Essex murders, he flew to Chicago, rented a car, and drove nine hundred miles to Vermont, where he dug up the murder kit.

Keyes' last victim was Samantha Koenig. He kidnapped her in Anchorage, Alaska, raped her, and murdered her. He was arrested in Texas while using Koenig's debit card. He confessed to her murder but killed himself in custody by slitting his wrists and strangling himself before he could go to trial.

While in Essex, check out Above Reality Hot Air Ballon rides. Since 2002, Above Reality Balloons has been flying over Vermont to give tourists memories to last a lifetime and get a hot air balloon ride off their bucket list.

BOSTON, MASSACHUSETTS

Albert DeSalvo—aka the Boston
Strangler
Kills: 13
Span of Activity: June 1962 to
January 1964

Fun Fact: He served as a military police sergeant

Boston is an amazing city, filled with historic sites, museums, fine universities, and parks. It's one of the coolest cities you could visit anywhere, especially if you're a drunk white guy. It possibly has more dive bars per capita than any city in the United States. Boston can aptly be described as a city of bleeding-heart liberals who actively want to kill you.

So after you visit Paul Revere's house or catch the Red Sox at Fenway, head on over to the Tam, one of the finest dive bars in Boston. If you tip right and keep your mouth shut, you'll do fine.

Albert DeSalvo was born on September 3, 1931, in Chelsea, Massachusetts. DeSalvo's father was a violent alcoholic. One afternoon, he knocked out all his wife's teeth and bent her fingers back until they broke in front of Albert and his siblings. He would also bring home sex workers and have sex with them in front of his wife and family. Sounds like fun, right? I hope he tipped well anyway. Apparently, all this shaped little Albert's view of the world in a slightly negative way.

It kind of goes without saying that DeSalvo was kind of a messed-up kid, although he did have fabulous hair. He began torturing animals and engaging in petty crime at a young age. DeSalvo was first arrested for battery and robbery when he was twelve years old.

In the 1960s, a series of similar sexual assaults began to occur in Boston. The rapist, also known as "the Measuring Man" or "the Green Man," had an insatiable appetite; he once raped four women in a single day. His vibe as the Measuring Man was to approach women in their homes and attempt to convince them they had a future in modeling. Then he'd "measure" them. Apparently, this incredibly well-thought-out scheme worked enough to get him through the door, and once he was in, he did whatever he wanted to his hapless victims.

At the same time, a killer nicknamed the Boston Strangler was haunting the city, killing thirteen single women between 1962 and 1964. Each of the women was raped in her apartment before being strangled with articles of clothing. The women were often posed in ridiculous ways for family members or police to find, letting everyone know the Boston Strangler was not only a murderer, he was also a huge asshole.

Several of the victims identified DeSalvo as the person who raped them. He was arrested, but only faced charges of robbery and sexual assault. He was not charged with any of the murders.

Albert DeSalvo received life in prison for the rapes. Shortly after, he escaped from Bridgwater State Hospital, which triggered a huge manhunt. Three days later, he turned himself in.

In 1973, an inmate in prison stabbed DeSalvo to death, despite his excellent head of hair. In theory, he was murdered for selling meth in prison at a predatory price; which, let's face it, is just plain dumb.

While it's unclear if DeSalvo murdered all thirteen women, it's certainly likely. Decades after his death, DNA from the Boston Strangler's final victim matched DeSalvo.

While in Boston, go check out Fenway Park, one of the most iconic baseball stadiums in the world. Fenway is the oldest ballpark in Major League Baseball, home to the Boston Red Sox and the famed Green Monster, as well as an alarming number of drunks with urine stains on their shorts. And just remember, it's no fun to be a Yankees fan. They suck.

PROVINCETOWN, MASSACHUSETTS

Tony Costa—aka the Cape Cod Cannibal
Kills: 4-8
Span of Activity: June 1966 to January 1969

Fun Fact: Costa worked as a babysitter

From Boston, one can take a ferry to Provincetown, one of the most beautiful places on Cape Cod. Historically, Provincetown has been a haven for the LGBTQ+ community for decades. Many call Provincetown "the last gay resort." Provincetown has the same overpriced parking, the same quaint bed & breakfasts, the same pedestrian main street, the same fudge shops, and the same easy access to Tommy Bahama stores as the rest of Cape Cod. A visit to Provincetown lets you know that gay folks can be just as lame as the straights. But still, in Provincetown, they say you can be who you want to be.

That's not always a good thing; just ask those who encountered Tony Costa.

Tony Costa was born in 1945. At age sixteen, he entered a Somerville, Massachusetts, apartment, and stood next to the bed of a sleeping teenage girl. She woke up and screamed. Costa ran away with quickness. Costa wasn't big on taking hints. He came back three days later and tried to drag the same girl out of her apartment.

This led to him being convicted of burglary and assault. He got a one-year suspended sentence and three years' probation, which is ridiculously lenient for doing something so bizarre and sexually aggressive. In 1963, he married and had three children. Drug use and insanity caused the marriage to crumble. Which, ironically, are the same reasons mine did.

But enough about me.

In June 1966, he met two hippie girls named Bonnie Williams and Diane Federoff. He took off with them on a cross-country road trip, ready for some good times. Neither was ever seen again.

In 1967, he shot a female friend with an arrow while hiking. When she survived, Costa pretty much said, "Oops, it was an accident," which apparently worked. Perhaps women getting shot with arrows while hiking with male friends is common in Cape Cod.

A week later, eighteen-year-old Sydney Monzon vanished from her home in Provincetown; her disappearance was reported to police, but no one had any idea what happened to her. By August, Costa had a new live-in lover, Susan Perry; she disappeared a week after they moved in together. Costa told his friends that she had "gone to Mexico."

Yeah. Right.

On January 24, 1969, Patricia Walsh and Mary Anne Wysocki disappeared on a visit to Provincetown. Investigators learned that Walsh and Wysocki had been hanging out with Costa while there. I mean, why not? The dude was cool, right? People thought it odd that Costa had their car, but he produced a bill of sale and said they "left for Canada."

I imagine the next woman he killed would have left for the Ivory Coast.

On February 8, 1969, a search was organized for the women. During the search, police found what remained of Susan Perry. She had been cut into eight pieces. Soon afterward, the dismembered bodies of Walsh, Wysocki, and Monzon were found buried in the same grave. All the women's hearts had been removed, and the remains were covered with human teeth marks.

Costa was arrested on suspicion of murder after detectives learned that the burial site was an area he used for growing marijuana. When interviewed by police, Costa kept changing his story and failed a polygraph test.

He was convicted on four counts of murder and was sentenced to life imprisonment. Four years later, Costa hanged himself in his cell.

While in Provincetown, check out one of the most notorious cruising spots in the world: the Dick Dock. For decades, men have gathered here once the sun goes down, because under the Dick Dock, there's a certain magic that happens.

Well, sometimes. Other times, it's just a certain burning sensation.

SPRINGFIELD, MASSACHUSETTS

Stewart Weldon
Kills: 3
Span of Activity: December 2017
to March 2018

Fun Fact: Many of Weldon's friends describe him as a ladies' man

After taking the ferry back to Boston, you could drive an hour west to Springfield, a historic town on the shores of the Connecticut River. I say you "could" but trust me, no one ever does. While Springfield is the third-largest city in Massachusetts, one could spend a lifetime in this fine state without ever having a reason to go.

The city was used as a major arsenal during the Revolutionary War. Springfield is the birthplace and home of beloved children's author Theodore Geisel, whom I'm sure you know as Dr. Seuss. One can only assume his writing style benefited from never having a reason to go outside.

Stewart Weldon was born in the Jamaica neighborhood of Queens, New York.

In 1996, at age nineteen, Weldon sexually assaulted a girl at gunpoint, and was arrested for sexual assault and convicted. Sometime after getting released, he was arrested again, this time on weapons charges and kidnapping. He was sentenced to three years' probation. A few years later, he was arrested for burglary and was sentenced to one year and one day in prison.

It may seem like this young man has lost his way, but where he was headed was much farther off the path.

Upon his release, Weldon moved to Springfield, Massachusetts, which definitely wasn't the best thing for this fine city, as Weldon continued to act like a total jerk. In 2010, he was arrested for attempting to break into a liquor store and served eighteen months in prison. In 2015, he was arrested for threatening people with a gun in a bar.

On May 27, 2018, while waiting at a red light, Weldon was pulled over by Springfield Police because of driving with a broken taillight. There was a woman in the back seat who told police she had been kidnapped by Weldon; he had her captive for a month and had been physically abusing her and raping her repeatedly. That really must have been an awkward experience for everyone involved.

Weldon was arrested. Shortly afterwards, his mom called the cops and said something in her house smelled super bad. When police searched the home, they found the bodies of three women. Odd, his mom didn't notice the smell of three rotting corpses until her son was arrested for kidnapping, but you know, moms are gonna mom.

Weldon was charged with three counts of first-degree murder, eight counts of strangulation, nine counts of aggravated rape, two counts of rape, five counts of aggravated kidnapping, and four counts of kidnapping. On September 30, 2021, Weldon was sentenced to three life terms in prison.

Springfield is perhaps best known as the birthplace of basketball and home of the Basketball Hall of Fame. The story goes that local physical education teacher James Naismith invented the sport to fill the gaps between football and baseball seasons. While there, don't forget to pay homage to Bob McAdoo. He was a bad man. But just on the court.

WOONSOCKET, RHODE ISLAND

Jeffrey Mailhot—aka the Road
Island Ripper
Kills: 3
Span of Activity: February 2003
to July 2004

An hour to the east of Springfield is Woonsocket, Rhode Island, known for its rich industrial heritage and Autumnfest, which celebrates the fall season (hence the name) with parades, crafts, and entertainment. Woonsocket is known for the Museum of Work and Culture, which chronicles the lives of the city's mill workers and immigrants. You know you're in New England when mill workers and immigrants are celebrated, and I don't mean that as an insult. Although many other things written about Woonsocket are incredibly insulting, so let's move on, shall we?

What was not cause for celebration was the birth of Jeffrey Mailhot on November 9, 1970. After graduating from Woonsocket High School, he got a job at a paper mill and moved into an apartment downtown. In Woonsocket, that's known as "living the dream."

In February 2003, Mailhot picked up Audrey L. Harris, a thirty-three-year-old sex worker, on the street. He brought her to her apartment and strangled her to death as soon as they got through the door. He kept her body in his apartment for a couple of days. He hadn't thought this whole thing through, apparently. Eventually, he watched an episode of *The Sopranos*, which gave him the idea of cutting her up with a saw in his bathtub. He put her remains in a trash bag and threw them in a dumpster.

In 2004, Mailhot murdered another sex worker, forty-two-year-old Christine C. Dumont. Same vibe here; he picked her up, brought her to his apartment, strangled her to death, dismembered her, and tossed her in a dumpster.

A few weeks later, Mailhot murdered Stacie K. Goulet after meeting her at a Fourth of July fireworks show. Just like the rest, he cut up her body and disposed of her remains.

In June 2004, Mailhot picked up a twenty-seven-year-old sex worker with the same goals in mind. Strangle, cut up, throw in a dumpster. If it ain't broke, why fix it? So the same vibe—he got her home and started to choke her out but she headbutted him and ran like crazy. When the police arrested Mailhot, he confessed to the murders and said he was glad he got caught because he knew he wouldn't be able to stop, which shows some great self-awareness. Good on you, Jeffrey.

Pretty sure all the women in Woonsocket were glad too.

Mailhot was charged with three counts of first-degree murder. He pleaded guilty and was sentenced to two terms of life imprisonment plus ten years. He now resides at the Rhode Island Maximum Security Prison in Cranston. Mailhot will be eligible for parole in 2047, when he is seventy-seven.

When in Woonsocket, check out Chan's, a place where you can experience fine Asian dining, while checking out some jazz and blues. If you've never had some egg rolls while checking out some sick blues riffs, I don't even want to know you.

NEW BRITAIN, CONNECTICUT

William Devin Howell—aka the
Sick Ripper
Kills: 7
Span of Activity: January through
October 2003

Fun Fact: Howell drove a van he called the "murder mobile"

To the east of Woonsocket sits New Britain, a city known for its access to major highways. How cool is that? New Britain has a history as a manufacturing hub and is nicknamed the Hardware City, in large part due to its connection to Stanley Black & Decker.

If you get tired of the snobby attitudes that permeate many areas of Connecticut, come to New Britain. Within minutes, you'll feel like you just got done with work at a rust belt factory and are heading home to split a two-pound ham steak with the family for dinner.

Howell grew up in Hampton, Virginia. He spent a lot of time in and out of jail for drug-related crimes. But come on, who hasn't? By the time he moved to Connecticut, he had convictions for larceny and burglary in Virginia.

In 2003, thirty-three-year-old Nilsa Arizmendi disappeared. Arizmendi's boyfriend was interviewed by police but was cleared after passing a polygraph test. He told investigators that Howell had stayed with him and Nilsa the night before she vanished, and he last saw her around 2:30 in the morning when she got into Howell's van.

Police seized his van and discovered that several of the seat cushions had been removed and blood was found soaked into the carpet on the floor of the car. Howell apparently wasn't expecting to get looked at this closely; either that or he really felt like the rug pulled the van's vibe together.

DNA taken determined that the blood sample from Howell's van was 99 percent certain to be a match to Nilsa.

Howell was charged at that time with first-degree manslaughter because there was no body. Howell stated the bloodstains were from a fight that Nilsa Arizmendi had in the van with her boyfriend. The old "blame the boyfriend" gambit partially worked, as Howell was sentenced to fifteen years in prison for manslaughter in the first degree.

But Howell's luck ended there. Just weeks after his sentencing, a hunter found human bones in an area Howell frequented, which he called his "garden." The remains of four more women were discovered there as well. Howell told his cellmate he kept one of the women's bodies in his van for two weeks because it was too cold outside to bury her.

That ain't right.

On November 17, 2017, Howell was sentenced to six consecutive life sentences after pleading guilty to the murders of six women. He cried and apologized to the families of the victims during sentencing, calling his actions "monstrous, cowardly, and selfish."

On your way out of New Britain, check out the New Britain Industrial Museum. Here, you can gaze with pride at exhibits featuring long hours, low wages, dangerous workplaces, and child labor. You aren't supposed to bring in booze, but no one checks.

BRIDGEPORT, CONNECTICUT

Emanuel Lovell Webb—aka the
East End Killer
Kills: 5+
Span of Activity: April 1990 to
June 1993

Fun Fact: Webb was employed as a security guard

Bridgeport is a city of over 144,000 residents, featuring vibrant parks, museums, and minor league sports. Bridgeport is also known for its history, including the invention of the electric plug outlet and the opening of the first Subway restaurant, two things our society simply couldn't do without.

Bridgeport is one of the most dangerous cities in Connecticut. Fifty percent of Bridgeport is Catholic, which means they're either victimized constantly by thugs or the Catholics are thugs, you be the judge. I know which way I'm leaning. One of the worst areas is called The Hollow. You might not be killed if you live there, but after a couple of weeks, you're going to wish you were.

On April 1, 1990, Bridgeport Police responded to a car on fire on a downtown street. Upon arrival, they found the charred remains of a woman in the back seat. She had been strangled. Male DNA was found on her body, leading authorities to suspect she had also been raped.

In 1992, police responded to a call and found the body of twenty-nine-year-old Minnie Sutton in her living room, her body covered with stab wounds. She had been raped and strangled. Her three-year-old son was in the home but was left unharmed.

Next, Elizabeth "Maxine" Gandy vanished without a trace. She was found topless in an abandoned building. Then, the father

of twenty-nine-year-old Sheila Etheridge found her body in her apartment after checking on her because he hadn't heard from her in a few days.

In the summer of 1994, thirty-six-year-old Evelyn Charity was found dead in her home. She had been strangled and stabbed to death and her Chevrolet Camaro was stolen.

Not long after, police arrested Webb, in large part because he was still stupidly in possession of her Camaro. Come on, man, you're slaughtering people all over the place and you're going to let a 1990 Camaro take you down? Take the bus, bro. Come on.

Webb admitted he killed Etheridge, but said he accidentally strangled her to death whilst the two were making the beast with two backs. He then panicked and stabbed her and ransacked the house to make it look like a robbery gone bad. Makes sense, right? Who wouldn't stab the corpse of a woman numerous times after you already "accidently" strangled her to death whilst screwing? We've all done it at least once.

Webb pleaded guilty to involuntary manslaughter, robbery, and motor vehicle theft, and was given a twenty-year sentence. He was paroled after only seven years in late 2001.

In 2005, Webb, who was finally free at last and ready to shine, moved back to Connecticut. He was busted for drug possession and failing to disclose his residency change, which violated his parole conditions. After he was arrested, he was required to submit a sample of his DNA. In early 2006, investigators found that DNA Webb submitted matched the murdered women he had killed in the '90s. To top it all off, detectives discovered records revealed Webb checked into a hospital for cuts to his hand the day after Gandy was killed. First, this dumbass is busted with the Camaro, *then* he was nailed for other murders because he didn't check in with his probation officer. This is the kind of thing that would really be embarrassing at a gathering of serial killers.

Webb was charged with Gandy's murder. Later that month, he was convicted and sentenced to sixty years in prison. Webb is incarcerated at the MacDougall-Walker Correctional Institution in Suffield. While Bridgeport authorities conclusively linked Webb to four murders, they suspect he could have claimed up to fifteen victims.

Hit Matty's Corner on the way out of town, or maybe on the way in if you're driving. This is one of the best dive bars with some of the strongest drinks you'll find anywhere. Just mind your manners and you'll do fine.

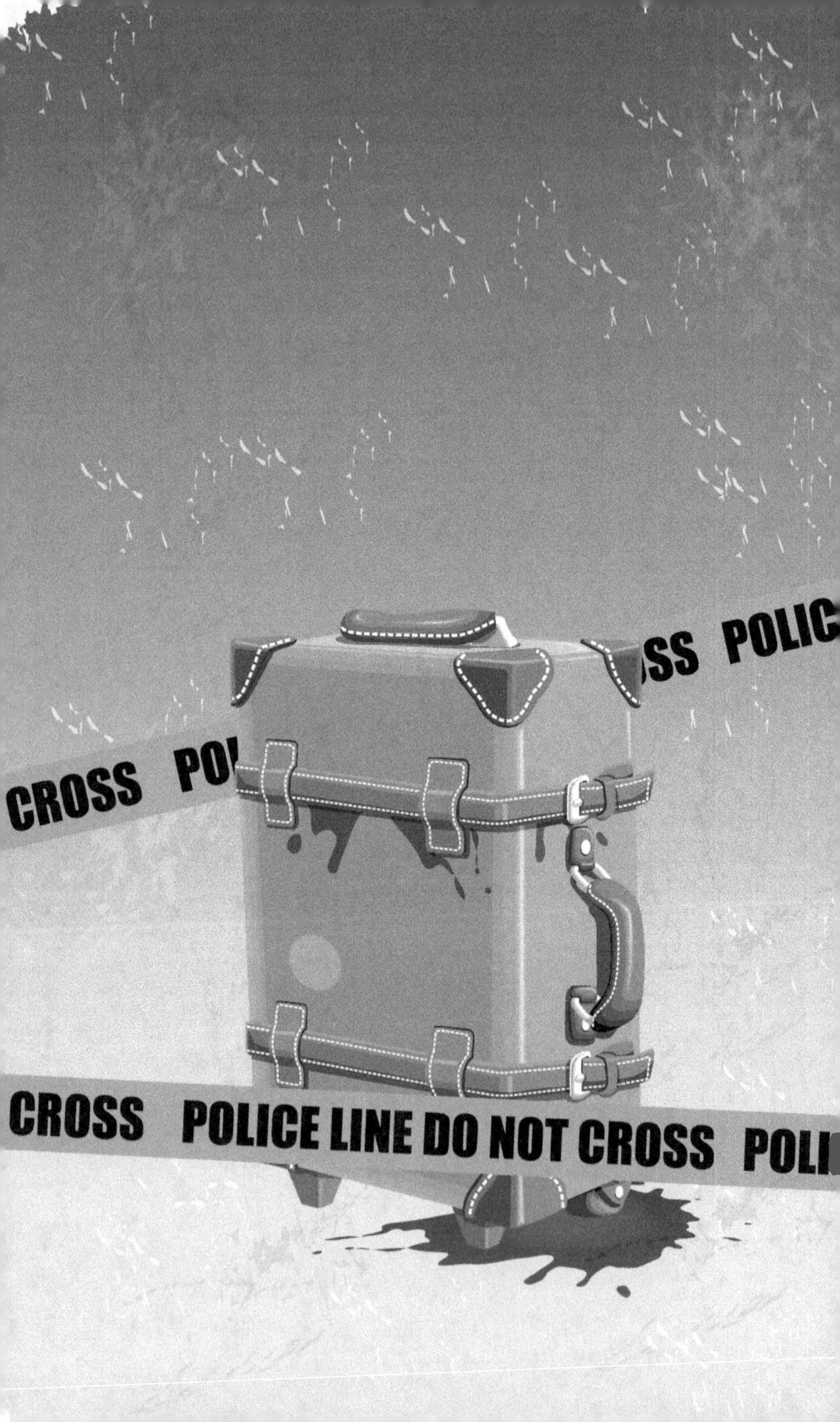
SS POLIC
CROSS POL
CROSS POLICE LINE DO NOT CROSS POLI

MID-EAST REGION

The Mid-East region of the United States—a place where New York thinks it's the center of the universe, Pennsylvania can't decide if it's East Coast or Midwest, and New Jersey remains deeply offended that you even asked. Delaware exists *mostly* as a tax haven, Maryland is still mad that everyone only cares about its crabs, and Washington, DC, is where people go to make bad decisions on a national scale.

New York, of course, dominates the region with its towering ego and bagels that inspire religious devotion. But venture upstate and you'll find a land of economically depressed towns where people say "the city" with a mix of reverence and resentment. Pennsylvania, meanwhile, features Pittsburgh and Philadelphia, two cities that are basically cultural cousins who hate each other, separated by an endless stretch of highway, lovingly referred to as "Pennsyltucky."

New Jersey, America's perpetual underdog, thrives on diners, turnpike rage, and the unshakable belief that everyone else is wrong about it (spoiler alert: they're not). Delaware remains a mystery, a state so small that people forget it exists until they have to register an LLC. Maryland, ever the seafood-obsessed sibling, insists that Old Bay seasoning is a personality trait, and DC, the country's capital, is a fascinating experiment in what happens when you put too many overachievers in one place and make sure they all disappoint you.

So, there you have it—the Mid-East. A region of contradictions, complaints, and the kind of passive-aggressive charm that could fuel a thousand Thanksgiving fights. It may not always make sense, but hey, at least you can get a decent sandwich.

NEW YORK CITY, NEW YORK

David Berkowitz—aka the Son of Sam
Kills: 6
Span of Activity: July 1976 to July 1977

Welcome to New York City, a charming little hamlet where the buildings are tall, the people are warm and inviting (just kidding), and the rats have been bulking up for summer. Whether you're here to take in the sights, catch a Broadway show, or simply test how long you can hold your breath in a subway station, there's something for everyone—assuming you enjoy spending too much money and standing in lines.

If you thought New York City in the '70s couldn't get worse, add a serial killer and Billy Martin, and you have a recipe for chronic hysteria. New York City in the 1970s was like that weird uncle who shows up to Thanksgiving reeking of gin and full of stories that should probably be run past a lawyer. It was a gritty, graffiti-covered Hellscape when Times Square was less "Disneyland for influencers" and more "hookers, heroin, and a guy selling watches out of his sock." The economy was in shambles, crime was through the roof, and landlords had this fun little habit of burning down their own buildings for insurance money. It was the kind of place where you didn't so much *live* as you *survived*, preferably while chain-smoking and wearing something suede and fringed.

And then, just when New Yorkers thought their biggest problem was getting mugged in broad daylight, along came David Berkowitz, a postal worker with a talking demon-dog problem. Between 1976 and 1977, the city was gripped by terror as he roamed the streets, targeting couples making out in parked cars (which, if you think about it, really feels like an attack on romance. *Who hurt you, David?*).

David Berkowitz, also known as the Son of Sam, is one of those delightful figures in American history who makes you question whether moving to Canada is really such a bad idea. Born in 1953, Berkowitz spent his early years as a run-of-the-mill awkward kid before blossoming into a full-blown serial killer—sort of the opposite of a glow-up.

He terrorized the Bronx, Flushing, and Queens with killings that had everyone rethinking late-night strolls and, more importantly, their choice of a parked car. He claimed he was acting on orders from a demonically possessed dog, which, if true, makes you wonder why no one ever interviews the dog in these cases. What exactly did this Labrador have to say? And more importantly, why aren't we funding more dog therapy programs?

His arrest in 1977 was a real testament to the power of good old-fashioned parking violations. That's right—New York City's most notorious murderer was caught because of a parking ticket. Let this be a lesson to us all: if you're going to be an unhinged lunatic, at least feed the meter.

Since being sentenced to life in prison, Berkowitz has found God (as they all do), changed his nickname to the Son of Hope (which, frankly, is a rebrand no one asked for), and spends his time writing letters about redemption. Because nothing says, "I've changed," like a handwritten note from a maximum-security prison.

But since you're in the Big Apple, you might want to see Times Square, a famous landmark you'll pretend to enjoy. While there, you'll see a dazzling display of advertisements so bright they'll be laser burnt into your retinas. Here, you can pay fifteen dollars for a hot dog while fending off a man in an off-brand Spider-Man costume who demands a photo with your wallet.

ROCHESTER, NEW YORK

Fun Fact: One suspect for these crimes is one of the Hillside Stranglers, Kenneth Bianchi, who worked as an ice cream vendor in Rochester at the time of the murders

Alphabet Murders
Kills: 3
Span of Activity: November 1971 to November 1973

Rochester—New York State's best-kept secret, mostly because no one's really looking for it. Nestled between Buffalo and Syracuse (two other places people try to avoid), Rochester is famous for its Kodak-era glory, its aggressive weather patterns, and the eerie realization that, despite living here for years, you somehow still don't know exactly what people do for fun.

Rochester is accessible by car, train, or an airport so small that your baggage claim experience will make you feel like you're in a hostage situation. Flying in? You'll enjoy the classic Rochester welcome of gray skies and a light drizzle that never quite stops. Driving? Well, just be prepared for the roads to be under construction no matter what time of year it is. And if you're taking Amtrak, congratulations! You've chosen the slowest possible way to get here that doesn't involve a horse.

Rochester is a city of contradictions: It has great museums, but no one really visits them. It has a scenic waterfront, but it's too cold to enjoy most of the year. It has a booming tech industry, but somehow, you'll still see a surprising number of people wearing Kodak jackets from the '90s. If you love unpredictable weather, heavy meals, and a city that refuses to acknowledge the passage of time, then congratulations—Rochester is the perfect place for you.

But besides mountains of lake-effect snow and RIT, Rochester is also home to one of the nation's gruesome unsolved serial murders.

If *Sesame Street* ever decided to do a true crime spin-off (which, honestly, would be a hit), Rochester, New York, would be the perfect setting. Back in the early 1970s, the city found itself in the grip of a serial killer with a disturbingly specific theme: all his victims had first and last names that started with the same letter—like Carmen Colón, Wanda Walkowicz, and Michelle Maenza. This is, of course, the kind of thing that makes you wonder if he was a murderer first or just a guy with obsessive tendencies who took things way too far.

Between 1971 and 1973, three young girls were found murdered, their bodies dumped in locations that just also happened to match the first letter of their names. It was like some twisted version of a children's word game, except instead of being fun, it was deeply horrifying. The pattern was obvious, which made it even more frustrating when the police were left grasping at straws. Who commits murders based on a naming system? And, more importantly, how had Rochester produced a serial killer *this* dedicated to organization?

At various points, the police had a few people in mind, including a guy named Miguel Colón (related to the first victim), and a serial killer and rapist named Joseph Naso, whose thing was also—you guessed it—killing women with matching initials. Naso really did himself no favors by keeping a handwritten list of victims. If you're going to be a criminal mastermind, at least don't be this bad at it. Despite a handful of promising leads, no one was ever charged, which means that even today, the Alphabet Murders remain unsolved—kind of like a deeply disturbing crossword puzzle no one could finish.

Though the killings stopped, the case has lived on in infamy, partly because people love a mystery and partly because the concept of an alliteration-obsessed serial killer is just so bizarre. The case has been featured in books, TV specials, and way too many internet deep dives written by people who probably should be focusing on their real jobs.

So, if you ever find yourself in Rochester, check out the Seabreeze Amusement Park, the fourth-oldest amusement park in America. While there, you can enjoy the experience of a meth-binging carnie locking you into a roller coaster by using a rusty conner pin.

PHILADELPHIA, PENNSYLVANIA

Marty Graham
Kills: 7
Span of Activity:1986 to 1987

Fun Fact: Graham was athletic and frequently played basketball with the neighborhood youth

Philadelphia—the land of brotherly love, historic landmarks, and a population that would fight a ghost if it looked at them wrong. Nestled between the cultural snobbery of New York and the political doom vortex of DC, Philly has all the charm of a blue-collar fever dream, complete with a scent that is one part soft pretzel and two parts subway mystery.

Philadelphia is best known for its cheesesteaks, which are essentially just meat, cheese, and bread but with a side of rage. You will be judged for how you order one, so learn the rules: it's Whiz wit (cheese sauce with onions) or Whiz wit'out (without onions). If you try to get fancy with it, say, by requesting provolone, you will be exiled immediately.

Other local delicacies include soft pretzels, which function as both food and an impromptu weapon, and scrapple, which is what happens when you take breakfast meat and remove any sense of dignity. Don't forget to wash it down with a glass of "wooder."

Philadelphia has a rich history, incredible food, and a collective personality that can only be described as a "guy yelling at traffic while holding a Wawa coffee." If you love culture, grit, and the feeling that a stranger might punch you for mispronouncing Schuylkill, then congratulations—this is the city for you!

If Philadelphia has given us anything, it's an endless supply of hoagies, a sports culture fueled entirely by rage, and a handful

of truly bizarre criminals. Enter Harrison "Marty" Graham, a man who managed to combine murder with hoarding in a way that even *Hoarders* producers would probably find excessive.

Harrison "Marty" Graham was born in Philadelphia on September 9, 1959, the eldest of five children. Graham was your average Philly guy—except for the part where he strangled women and then forgot about them in his North Philadelphia apartment, like leftovers he swore he'd eat later. Unlike most serial killers, who at least have the decency to hide their crimes, Marty just... didn't. His idea of covering things up was piling garbage on top of decomposing bodies, which, shockingly, did not work.

Early in his life, he was diagnosed with mental disorders that required him to take lengthy stays in facilities. And if you know anything about Philly during the 1960s, it was like David Lynch once said: "Philadelphia, Pennsylvania, is my biggest influence. There is something about the mood here. The fear, insanity, corruption, filth, despair, violence in the air was so beautiful to me." (Lynch 2014) One could imagine that if Graham was spending time in mental health facilities during that time, it must have primed him for his weird future hobbies.

But by the 1970s, the "me" decade, Graham had a different outlook. He entered the workforce, moved out of his parents' house, and embarked on his newfound lust for life. And by "lust for life," I mean a constant flow of drugs, pimps, and prostitutes.

By the time the '80s rolled around, he wasn't one for the yuppie way of living. Instead, he rented his apartment in a beat-up part of town.

In 1987, Graham was evicted from his apartment because— brace yourself—it smelled *terrible*. Now, a bad-smelling apartment in Philly is nothing new (have you *been* to a South Street bathroom?), but this was next level. Neighbors had been complaining for months, assuming it was the result of Philadelphia's usual suspects: bad plumbing, aggressive rodents, or possibly a forgotten Wawa sandwich left out since the Bicentennial.

When the landlord finally forced Graham out, he left behind more than just a security deposit dispute. Inside his apartment, authorities found seven bodies, casually strewn about like old furniture, which, to be fair, was *also* still in there. Imagine being the poor cop who opened that door expecting to find some abandoned junk, only to walk straight into a DIY morgue.

Once caught, Graham did what any rational person would do— he claimed innocence. His defense? He was just a hoarder, not a murderer. Yes, you read that correctly. His argument was essentially: *Sure, I kept piles of trash, but I definitely didn't put the bodies there!* Because, of course, nothing makes more sense than *accidentally* collecting corpses like they're expired coupons from Rite Aid.

Shockingly, the jury did not buy this. He was convicted of multiple murders and sentenced to life in prison, presumably far away from any storage space.

But while you're in Philly, feel free to take in the Liberty Bell. Here, you can marvel at a broken bell inside a glass box while someone behind you loudly explains how "we should just fix it already."

KING OF PRUSSIA, PENNSYLVANIA

John Eichinger
Kills: 4
Span of Activity: July 1999 to March 2005

Fun Fact: Eichinger was an enthusiastic Dungeons and Dragons player and participated in local chess tournaments

If you ever find yourself in King of Prussia, Pennsylvania, chances are you made a wrong turn on the way to Philadelphia or you've been lured in by the siren song of capitalism, also known as the King of Prussia Mall. The town—if we can even call it that—exists in a state of perpetual retail therapy, a swirling vortex of shopping plazas, office parks, and hotel chains with a commitment to hospitality so strong it borders on sinister.

The name "King of Prussia" suggests grandeur, perhaps a sprawling kingdom of cobblestone streets and regal history; in reality, it's a large suburb with the aesthetic appeal of a well-maintained parking lot. The name itself comes from a tavern, the King of Prussia Inn, which once served weary travelers along the old Philadelphia Road. The inn is still there, though now marooned on a traffic island like an old fisherman left stranded by the tide of urban sprawl.

Born in 1972, John Eichinger looked like the kind of guy who might help you move a couch or explain the finer points of a *Star Wars* movie you didn't ask about. A grocery store employee by trade, he lived the kind of quiet, unassuming life that makes neighbors say, "He seemed nice," when the news inevitably breaks. But beneath his ordinary exterior was a festering resentment, the kind that twists rejection into something deadly.

Eichinger's crimes were not elaborate nor were they the work of some criminal mastermind. Instead, they were brutal and tragically predictable: a man rejected, a man unable to cope, a man who decided that if he couldn't have the women he wanted, then no one else could either.

Between 1999 and 2005, Eichinger killed four people, each murder stemming from his inability to handle rejection. His first victim was Jennifer Still, a young woman a man had feelings for but who, like many women before her, made the fatal mistake of not reciprocating them. Instead of sulking into a pint of Ben & Jerry's like the rest of us, Eichinger stabbed her to death.

For six years, he managed to exist unnoticed, blending into the suburban monotony, until he struck again in 2005. This time, it was Heather Greaves, another woman who had rejected him, along with her three-year-old daughter, and her sister, Lisa. The sheer brutality of these murders—three victims in one day, including a child—shattered the illusion that King of Prussia was just a shopping mecca and not also the occasional site of pure evil.

Eichinger wasn't some criminal genius who outwitted the police for decades. No, his downfall was as mundane as the setting of his crimes. Shortly after the Greaveses' murders, he confessed to a coworker, perhaps mistaking casual workplace chatter for an appropriate venue to reveal a quadruple homicide. The police arrested him, and in a move that surprised exactly no one, he quickly confessed.

In 2005, he was sentenced to death, which in Pennsylvania means he now resides in a prison where he'll likely live out his days because the State hasn't actually executed anyone since the days when flip phones were considered cutting edge.

While in town check out the King of Prussia Mall, which is what happens when you give an architect unlimited square footage and a deep distrust of the outdoors. It is one of the largest malls in the United States, which means you can lose both your dignity and your will to live somewhere between Nordstrom and the Cheesecake Factory. Every store you've ever heard of is here, including some you'd assume went out of business years ago. The Apple Store is always packed, and there is inevitably a child weeping outside the LEGO Store, overwhelmed by the weight of possibility.

ATLANTIC CITY, NEW JERSEY

Eastbound Strangler—aka the Atlantic City Serial Killer
Kills: 4
Span of Activity: 2006

Fun Fact: a reward of $25,000 for information remains unclaimed.

Atlantic City, New Jersey, is what happens when someone describes Las Vegas to a group of deeply confused urban planners who then attempt to recreate it using only expired coupons and broken dreams. Nestled along the Jersey Shore, this once glamorous resort town now serves as a poignant reminder that no matter how much money you pour into the slot machines, the house always wins, and by house, I mean the State of New Jersey, which is barely keeping the lights on.

Steel Pier offers carnival rides and attractions, perfect if you've ever wanted to experience the thrill of almost dying while strapped into a decades-old roller coaster operated by a man with an eyepatch. If you prefer your amusement without a side of motion sickness, Ripley's Believe It or Not! Museum is there to remind you that yes, things can always get weirder.

What Atlantic City also has, besides casinos and boardwalks, is a serial killer named after it. Atlantic City, New Jersey, is not a place typically associated with mystery. Any secrets this town may have once had have long since been washed away by a combination of saltwater, spilled margaritas, and poor life choices. But in November 2006, something truly unsettling happened that couldn't be explained away by an unfortunate night at the blackjack table or a bad encounter with gas station sushi.

That something was the Eastbound Strangler.

Picture this: a drained marsh behind the Golden Key Motel, one of those charming roadside establishments that offers all the ambiance of a police interrogation room, with decor that screams "someone *definitely* died here!" Probably recently. It was in this scenic location that a group of women, all strangled and left barefoot, were found lying face down in a row, eerily positioned, as if whoever did this had a real passion for symmetry.

Each woman had worked as a sex worker, a profession that Atlantic City (and most of the world) likes to pretend doesn't exist while actively depending on it. They had been placed, deliberately, facing east—as if awaiting sunrise, or perhaps just an Uber out of New Jersey.

The motel, of course, had no shortage of characters who could be suspects. The kind of place where someone could rent a room for thirty bucks and still feel overcharged, the Golden Key catered to those who needed to disappear for a night, whether from their wives, their drug dealers, or the police.

The Atlantic City Police, bless their hearts, launched an investigation that was about as effective as trying to mop up a hurricane with a Swiffer. They looked at a number of suspects, including a handy local pimp—because of course there was one—and a few other men who seemed, let's say, not entirely innocent. But like most things in Atlantic City, the case never quite came together.

One of the leading theories was that the killer might have been someone passing through—a trucker, a drifter, or a man who had bet his life savings on a losing roulette spin and decided to take up murder as a side hobby. Another was that this was the work of someone local, a man who blended into the background of Atlantic City so seamlessly that no one thought twice about him.

The problem was, and remains, that Atlantic City is exactly the kind of place where people disappear all the time. Sometimes by choice, sometimes because they run out of cash, and sometimes because they meet the wrong person in the wrong motel.

Despite the keystone cops' level effort, the Eastbound Strangler was never caught. Theories abound—was it a serial killer passing through? A local with a taste for something more sinister than saltwater taffy? Or, as some conspiracy theorists like to suggest, someone with enough power and influence to make the case quietly disappear, much like the victims themselves?

Atlantic City, of course, has moved on. The Golden Key Motel was demolished, replaced by something just as forgettable, and the Boardwalk crowds continue their usual routines of losing money, eating suspicious seafood, and making life decisions they'll regret before checkout.

But if you find yourself in Atlantic City, maybe staying in a motel that smells vaguely of lonely nights, take a look around. Because someone out there, someone who once walked these same neon-lit streets, got away with murder. And in a town built on risk and reward, that might just be the biggest jackpot of all.

Before you leave, check out the Atlantic City Boardwalk. It's four miles of deep-fried optimism, lined with souvenir shops selling shirts that say things like What Happens in Atlantic City Stays in Your Medical Records. Here, you can purchase everything from knockoff sunglasses to saltwater taffy that will glue your teeth together like an adhesive experiment gone wrong.

TRENTON, NEW JERSEY

Anthony Balaam—aka the Trenton
Strangler
Kills: 4
Span of Activity: October 1994 to
July 1996

Fun Fact: Balaam will become eligible for parole in 2116.

If you've found yourself in Trenton, New Jersey, I can only assume one of three things has happened:

1. You took a wrong turn on the way to literally anywhere else.
2. You have a court date.
3. You lost a bet.

Nestled along the Delaware River like an old Band-Aid that refuses to float away, Trenton is the state capital, which is adorable when you consider that the only people who actually want to be here are politicians, and even they seem to leave as soon as their meetings are over.

The good news is, Trenton is accessible by train. The bad news is, you have to get off the train. If you arrive by car, you'll be greeted by the famous bridge that boldly proclaims Trenton Makes, The World Takes, a slogan so outdated it might as well read, *We Invented the Fax Machine and Haven't Done Much Since.*

Trenton has history, sure, but so does every place that existed before 1980. You could visit the Old Barracks Museum, where Revolutionary War soldiers once fought to liberate the land that would eventually become the setting for an Arby's parking lot brawl. If you're a fan of George Washington (or just someone who enjoys mildly disappointing attractions), you can check out Washington's Crossing, where he heroically rowed across the Delaware River to escape Trenton's high cost of colonial living.

And, of course, there's the State Capitol Building, where you can watch democracy in action—or at least watch a group of officials pretend to care about fixing the pothole you just hit on the way in.

When people hear the words *serial killer*, their minds often drift to cinematic depictions of criminal masterminds—calculating villains who outwit police for years, leaving cryptic notes, and constructing elaborate murder dens that, quite frankly, require more dedication than most people put into their day jobs.

And then there's Anthony Balaam.

Known as the Trenton Strangler, Balaam's story is neither cinematic nor particularly complex. It is, however, a deeply depressing reflection of Trenton, New Jersey—a city where even the serial killers seem to be phoning it in.

Born in 1965, Anthony Balaam grew up in Trenton, which is sort of like growing up in a place that never quite finished being built but still insists on calling itself a city. Like many criminals before him, Balaam's early life was filled with indicators—petty theft, burglaries, and a general disregard for the concept of personal property. The kind of guy who might steal your wallet and then help you look for it.

By the late 1990s, Balaam had graduated from small-time crime to something much worse. Between 1994 and 1996, he attacked and strangled four women, all sex workers, in Trenton's less-than-scenic neighborhoods. His crimes, grim and methodical, followed a pattern—he would assault his victims, strangle them, and leave their bodies discarded like an afterthought; which, in a way, is how Trenton treats most of its problems.

Balaam was caught in 1996, which makes sense because his version of serial killing lacked any of the subtlety or strategy that allows more infamous murderers to elude capture. He wasn't sending taunting letters to the press. He wasn't playing cat-and-mouse games with detectives. He was just committing horrible crimes and hoping no one would notice.

Spoiler: they noticed.

DNA evidence linked him to the crimes, and when police confronted him, he confessed almost immediately, as if he had simply run out of excuses. His arrest didn't exactly shake Trenton to its core, largely because Trenton has seen worse. This is a city where crime is as common as potholes, and people have come to accept both as permanent fixtures of daily life.

Balaam was sentenced to life in prison, where he remains to this day, hopefully reflecting on the many, many terrible decisions that led him there. Unlike some serial killers, whose names become legends whispered in true crime documentaries, Balaam has largely faded into obscurity.

This is, perhaps, the final insult—if you're going to commit horrific crimes, the least you can do is be memorable. But Balaam, much like Trenton itself, is a name most people don't remember until they have no choice.

What does one take away from the story of Anthony Balaam? That Trenton is a city where even serial killers don't make national headlines? That crime, in certain places, is so routine it barely registers? Or that maybe, just maybe, we should all reconsider our life choices before we find ourselves in a motel off Route 1, contemplating our next move?

Either way, Trenton continues on, its reputation unchanged, its slogan still boldly claiming that Trenton Makes, The World Takes. And in the case of Anthony Balaam, the world took exactly what it expected from Trenton—another grim footnote in a city that never quite makes the history books for anything good.

For those who enjoy a good existential crisis, check out the New Jersey State Museum before you leave. The taxidermized animals stare blankly into the void alongside prehistoric fossils, which, like many Trenton residents, haven't moved in decades.

BEAR, DELAWARE

Steven Brian Pennell—aka the Route 40 Killer
Kills: 2–5
Span of Activity: November 1987 to September 1988

Fun Fact: Pennell represented himself in court

Bear, Delaware—a place that sounds like it was named after a thrilling encounter with a wild animal, but it was actually named after a tavern. Which, honestly, makes sense. This is the kind of place you drive through on the way to somewhere else, look around, and think, *Well, at least there's a Target.*

Located in New Castle County, Bear isn't exactly a destination. It's more of an accidental location, like when your GPS malfunctions and you suddenly find yourself in the parking lot of a Wawa with no clear idea of how you got there. But if, for some reason, you do find yourself in Bear, don't worry—I've put together this guide to help you navigate the experience!

If you know anything about Delaware (which, let's be honest, you probably don't), you know that it's not exactly a hotbed of serial killer activity. People come to Delaware to register their LLCs, avoid sales tax, and, presumably, question their life choices. It's the kind of place where the most exciting thing to happen in a given year is the new Royal Farms opening.

And yet, in the late 1980s, Delaware produced its very own serial killer—Steven Brian Pennell, also known as the Route 40 Killer. His crimes were horrifying, his methods brutal, and his decision to commit multiple murders in a state where literally everyone knows each other was, frankly, one of the dumbest moves in serial killer history.

Born in 1957, Pennell was the classic guy you wouldn't notice if you were trapped in an elevator with him for three hours. He was an electrician, a family man, and the type of person who probably spent way too much time organizing his tools. But beneath his mundane, beige existence, he harbored a darker side—one that made even Delaware, a state famous for nothing, take notice.

Between 1987 and 1988, Pennell abducted, tortured, and murdered at least two women, though authorities believe the number was actually five. His hunting ground? Route 40, a stretch of highway in Northern Delaware best known for gas stations, strip malls, and the type of motels where you check in using a fake name and a deep sense of shame.

Unlike more infamous serial killers who spent years taunting the police with cryptic letters and elaborate schemes, Pennell was caught in a way that can only be described as spectacularly idiotic. In 1988, police were already on edge due to the string of brutal murders along Route 40, so they did something revolutionary: they sent out an undercover female officer to pose as a sex worker.

Enter Steven Brian Pennell.

Like an absolute moron, he picked up the undercover officer— in a blue van, no less, because nothing says subtlety like a man driving a vehicle that looks like it was purchased exclusively for the purpose of kidnapping. When she got into his van (which, by the way, had blue carpeting that matched fibers found on the victims because why not make it easier for the cops?), she noticed it was essentially straight out of a serial killer starter kit—restraints, torture tools, and a vibe that screamed, "I do terrible things in my spare time!"

The officer got a sample of the van's carpeting. Shocking twist: it was a match! And from there, Pennell's downfall was inevitable. Police obtained a warrant, searched his home, and found even more incriminating evidence, including a book on serial killers because of course he owned one. As a sidenote, by definition, you also own such a book now, but this book is *different* and only purchased by good, intelligent people such as yourself.

During his trial, Pennell, who, up until this point, had already proven himself to be as bright as a broken lightbulb, decided to represent himself.

That's right. A man with no legal experience thought, *You know what? I've totally got this.*

Spoiler: he did not, in fact, have this.

In an astonishing display of self-sabotage, he requested the death penalty, making him Delaware's first serial killer to be executed. His logic? Some nonsense about accepting his fate or finding peace or whatever killers tell themselves when they realize they are really bad at this whole "not getting caught" thing.

If you enjoy the great outdoors but don't want to be too challenged by it, Lums Pond is the place for you. Check it out before you leave. There's a pond (shocking, I know), hiking trails, and even a zipline course, because nothing says adventure like dangling over a body of water that is probably sixty percent algae. If you're lucky, you might see some wildlife, but the most common creatures you'll encounter are people in athleisure who have deeply overestimated their fitness levels.

SUITLAND, MARYLAND

Suitland Murderer
Kills: 5–9
Span of Activity: October 1986 to
January 1987

Suitland, Maryland—a place that sounds like it was named after a discount Men's Warehouse but, in reality, offers neither suits nor land that anyone particularly wants to claim. Located just outside Washington, DC, Suitland exists in that strange suburban purgatory where crime is a little too high, housing is a little too overpriced, and the only thing people truly agree on is that they'd rather be somewhere else.

But if fate (or a particularly cruel GPS) has led you here, don't panic. This should help you navigate you through with minimal trauma.

Yes, the US Census Bureau is based here, which means Suitland is technically responsible for counting every single person in the country—a bold task for a place that struggles to count the number of potholes in its own streets. There are no guided tours (outrageous, I know), but if you stand outside long enough, you might spot a government employee questioning every life decision they've ever made.

If you love the thrill of near-death experiences, take a drive down Suitland Parkway—a road that's equal parts scenic and terrifying. Originally built to provide military access to DC, it now provides high-speed access to road rage, aggressive lane changes, and the occasional fender bender that somehow backs up traffic for six hours.

Of course, there's the Suitland Murderer, because no mid-tier crime-ridden suburb is complete without its very own serial killer. While most towns would prefer to be known for something a little more wholesome (say, a beloved local diner or a quirky town festival), Suitland went with murder. Because of course it did.

Every serial killer has a thing—a creepy calling card, a bizarre obsession, something that sets them apart. Unfortunately, the Suitland Murderer's thing was simply existing in Suitland, which is already punishment enough.

Like many serial killers, his crimes were brutal, his methods horrifying, and his ability to evade capture depressingly effective. For a while, at least. The details of his life, much like the town he haunted, are bleak, uninspiring, and littered with the kind of choices that make you question humanity.

Between the late 1990s and early 2000s, a string of murders in Suitland made it clear that someone had taken up serial killing as a full-time hobby. The victims—mostly women—were found in varying states of brutality, with each crime scene telling the same grim story: a man who enjoyed violence, operated with disturbing precision, and somehow still thought Suitland was the best place to commit his crimes.

The murder locations? The kinds of places that already came with a certain level of built-in danger: abandoned buildings, darkened streets, and motel parking lots that looked like they doubled as crime scenes on a good day.

Alton Alsono Best was identified as a potential suspect because he was arrested for the murder of an unrelated girl. Conspiracy hounds tied Best to the killings because after he was arrested, the killings stopped. But remember: correlation isn't always causation.

On your way out of Suitland, one would be remiss if they didn't stop into Andrews Cocktail Lounge, where they proudly serve both Chinese and American food. Every Friday is ladies' night!

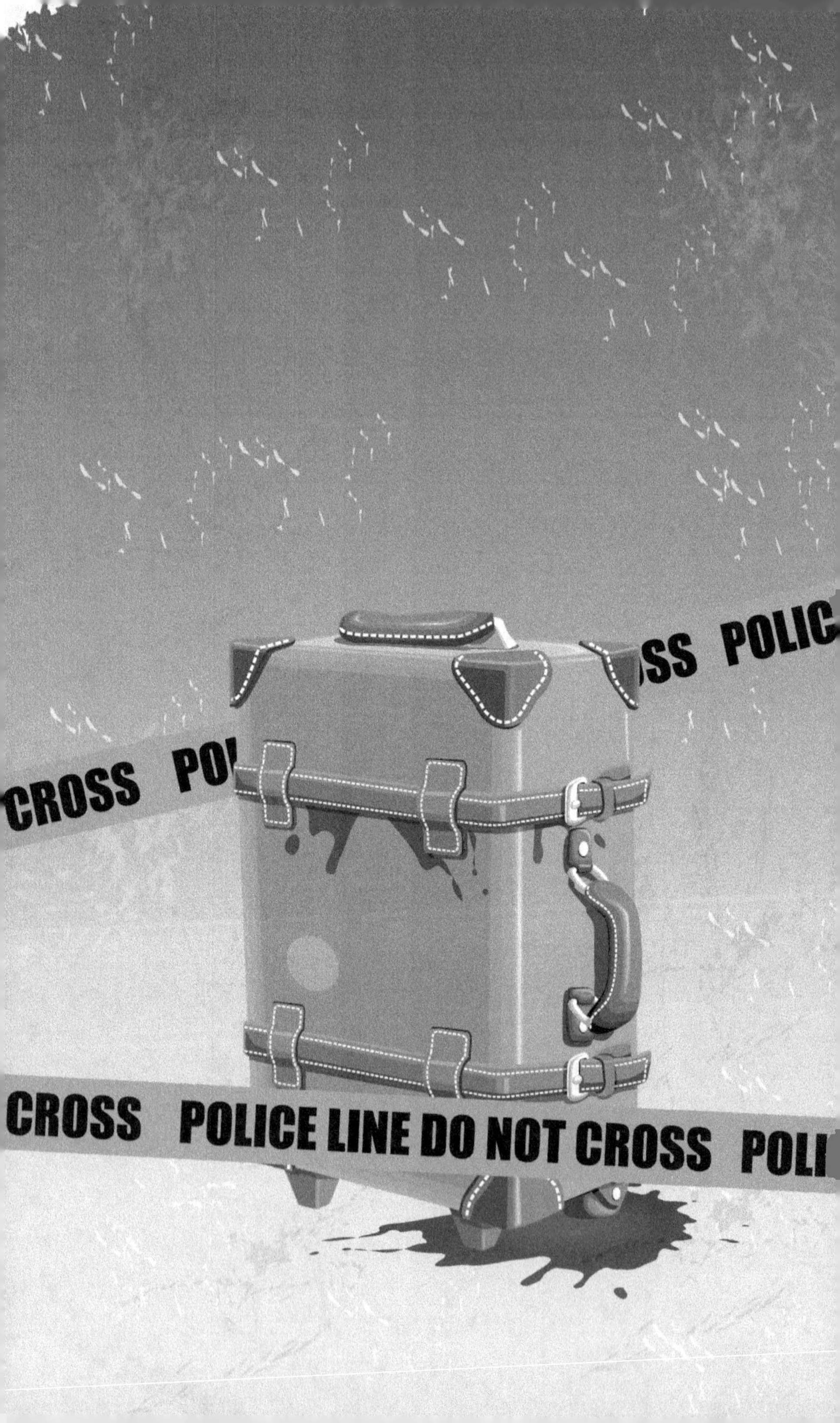
SS POLIC
CROSS POL
CROSS POLICE LINE DO NOT CROSS POLI

DISTRICT OF COLUMBIA

John Allen Muhammad—aka the Beltway Sniper, the DC Sniper
Kills: 17
Span of Activity: 2002

Washington, DC—the beating heart of American democracy, the grand stage for history, and the only place where you can be run over by a motorcade and then ticketed for jaywalking. As the nation's capital, DC attracts millions of visitors every year, all eager to see where *exactly* things went wrong.

But before you embark on your pilgrimage to the land of bureaucracy, overpriced coffee, and monuments that require *so much* walking, let me help you through the experience so you can plan accordingly—or at least prepare to be emotionally exhausted.

Home to Congress and one of the nation's highest crime rates (@thevisualcapitalist 2024), which, some might say are the same thing, Capitol Hill is a beautiful area filled with stunning architecture and *theoretical* democracy. Tours are available, but you won't be able to get anywhere important unless your uncle is a senator. Most people take a quick photo, sigh dramatically, then wander off in search of a bar.

Washington, DC, has seen its fair share of disasters—government shutdowns, traffic circles designed by sadists, and the time someone tried to make "fetch" happen at a Georgetown cocktail party. But none of these compares to the three-week reign of terror in 2002 when John Allen Muhammad, along with his teenage accomplice, Lee Boyd Malvo, decided to turn the nation's capital into his personal shooting gallery.

A failed businessman, a disgraced soldier, and an all-around terrible human being, Muhammad was not just your run-of-the-mill murderer. He was a man with a plan, albeit one that unraveled faster than a cheap suit in a rainstorm.

Born in 1960 in Louisiana, John Allen Muhammad started out as John Allen Williams, but like many people who make *deeply questionable* choices, he changed his name—presumably to avoid being associated with his own terrible past. A Gulf War veteran with a chip on his shoulder the size of the Pentagon, he had a history of failed marriages, financial instability, and a talent for making *everyone* around him uncomfortable.

At some point, Muhammad decided that instead of just being an everyday failure, he would go for the *full* villain origin story. He kidnapped his own kids, fled to Antigua for reasons that remain unclear, and somewhere along the way, picked up a seventeen-year-old sidekick, Lee Boyd Malvo, because nothing says *stable adult* like dragging a teenager into your criminal ambitions.

In October 2002, Muhammad and Malvo began what can only be described as a murder road trip, crisscrossing the DC metro area in a converted Chevrolet Caprice. A car that would later become Exhibit A in How Not to Be a Criminal Mastermind. Armed with a modified rifle and a sense of purpose only two deeply unhinged people could understand, they carried out ten murders and several more attempted killings, all from the trunk of their car.

And here's the thing: no one knew what the Hell was happening. People were getting shot while doing completely mundane activities—pumping gas, grocery shopping, sitting on a bench. Suddenly, the entire region was living in fear. Parents zigzagged in parking lots, people ducked behind their cars at gas stations, and someone probably considered ordering groceries for delivery before realizing it was 2002 and that technology did not exist yet.

For three weeks, absolute chaos. And, unlike most serial killers who keep their motives cryptic, Muhammad actually had a goal: terrorize the area so much that authorities would pay him millions of dollars to stop. Which was a plan so delusional it makes pyramid schemes look like Nobel-winning economics.

For someone who successfully evaded police for weeks, Muhammad's downfall was impressively dumb. The pair had been living out of their very obvious blue Chevrolet Caprice, which they had modified to function as a makeshift sniper's nest. Of course, if you're going to commit highly publicized crimes, you should definitely not invest in a hideout, a safe house, or literally *any* alternative to "just sleeping in your murder vehicle."

After an exhaustive investigation—and one very helpful tip from an exasperated truck driver—the police finally tracked the car to a Maryland rest stop, where they found both killers peacefully sleeping inside. That's right—they were napping. After paralyzing an entire region with fear, these two evil masterminds were taken down in the least dramatic way possible. No last stand, no high-speed chase, just two guys in a car who forgot that maybe they should keep moving.

Muhammad's trial was an absolute spectacle, mostly because he chose to represent himself, as all true narcissists do. His defense strategy seemed to consist of vague denials, courtroom theatrics, and absolutely no legal training whatsoever. Unsurprisingly, it did not go well. He was sentenced to death and executed in 2009.

Meanwhile, Malvo, the teenage sidekick who had clearly been manipulated, tried a different approach: he cooperated, showed remorse, and avoided the death penalty. Now serving life in prison, Malvo spends his days reflecting on the many,

many, many mistakes that led him from "angsty teen" to "accomplice in a murder spree."

It takes a lot to make DC more backstabbing, selfish, and terrorizing, but for a period in 2002, Muhammad and Malvo did just that.

Before leaving our nation's capital, take a few minutes to check out the Saint John Paul II National Shrine, dedicated to the worship of God and to furthering devotion to Saint John Paul II. When you're done, let us know if you feel any different. If not, keep on reading this book.

SOUTHEAST REGION

So, you've decided to venture into the Southeast. In this region, sweet tea is legally considered a form of currency, and "bless your heart" can mean either "you're adorable" or "I hope you fall into an abandoned well." You'll sweat through your shirt before you even finish reading this, but that's part of the charm, right?

It's a large region featuring many states, such as:

Kentucky—Bourbon, Bluegrass, and Questionable Horse Names
Ah, Kentucky, home of the Derby, bourbon strong enough to blind a horse, and a state economy mysteriously dependent on both fried chicken and professional wrestling. Louisville likes to pretend it's cosmopolitan, while the rest of the state prefers to wrestle with existential crises (and each other) in parking lots.

West Virginia—the Land of Accidental Whitewater Rafting
It is a place where the roads are made entirely of switchbacks and potholes, and every gas station has a "best biscuits in the state" sign. If you enjoy extreme sports, like driving, this is your place. Also, don't be alarmed if the locals immediately try to feed you something deep fried and call you "kin."

Virginia—The Ex That Can't Let Go
Virginia, the birthplace of America, and by that, I mean home to people who will remind you every five minutes that George Washington peed here once. It's a little bit South, a little bit North, and I'm one hundred percent convinced it's the most important state in the country. Richmond is a whole vibe;

Confederate statues and craft beer coexisting like an awkward divorced couple at Thanksgiving.

North Carolina—Barbecue Wars and Beach Traffic
North Carolina is best known for being unable to agree on what barbecue actually is. You have your Eastern-style vinegar people, your Lexington tomato people, and a few lost souls in the mountains who think barbecue is just "whatever fits in a smoker." Raleigh pretends it's Silicon Valley, Charlotte is trying to be Atlanta, and Asheville is where the hippies went to die.

South Carolina—Where Mosquitoes Are Considered Pets
If you've ever wanted to sweat through your socks while eating boiled peanuts in a swamp, welcome to South Carolina. Charleston is objectively gorgeous, but it's also where wealthy people move when they want to feel historic without actually reading history. Myrtle Beach is a place best visited while heavily intoxicated—preferably before noon.

Arkansas—Walmart's Personal Playground
Ever wonder where Walmart was born? No? Well, too bad. Arkansas is a land of natural beauty (seriously, it's stunning), occasionally interrupted by a Dollar General every three miles. The Ozarks are great for hiking, and Little Rock is... well, it's there.

Tennessee—Country Music and Bachelorette Parties
Nashville is where dreams of country stardom come to die in a sea of overpriced cowboy boots and "woo, girl!" bachelorette parties. Memphis is a bluesy working-class social experiment, best experienced with ribs in one hand and a cocktail in the other. The rest of the state is moonshine, mountains, and an unsettling number of roadside fireworks stands.

Mississippi—A Museum of the 19th Century
Mississippi is a place where time has moved selectively. The food is outstanding, the hospitality is suspiciously friendly,

and the Wi-Fi is still buffering from 2013. If you're looking for literary history, Oxford has a Faulkner thing going on—just be prepared for locals to tell you stories that may or may not be legally considered fiction.

Alabama—Football, Fried Food, and the Feud with Auburn

There are two things that matter in Alabama: college football and deep-fried everything. If you don't have an opinion on the Alabama-Auburn rivalry, someone will assign you one. Birmingham has a thriving food scene while Mobile is basically New Orleans' weird little cousin.

Georgia—Coca-Cola and the Art of Passive Aggression

Atlanta is a city where traffic laws are mere suggestions, and somehow, everyone simultaneously loves and hates living there. The rest of Georgia is divided between genteel Southern charm and people who unironically eat peanuts in their Coke. Savannah is haunted—both by ghosts and the consequences of your own bad decisions.

Louisiana—Where Chaos is a Lifestyle

New Orleans alone is a reason to visit Louisiana, assuming you enjoy beignets, jazz, and making choices you'll regret by morning. The state is drunk with Cajun food, alligator sightings, and humidity so thick you could cut it with a knife (which, coincidentally, most locals carry).

Florida—America's Drunk Uncle

Florida is not just a state; it's a lawless swamp masquerading as a theme park. Miami is an international metropolis where everyone is beautiful and overdressed while the rest of Florida is either theme parks, alligators, or men named Randy getting arrested for wrestling said alligators. The further south you go, the more likely you are to stumble into a retirement community where golf carts outnumber cars.

LONDON, KENTUCKY

Donald Harvey—aka the Angel
of Death
Kills: 37- 87
Span of Activity: May 1970 to
March 1987

London, Kentucky—not to be confused with that other London with the Queen, Big Ben, and people who somehow make bad weather seem sophisticated. No, this London is nestled deep in Laurel County, where the accents are thicker than the gravy, and the most exciting event is an annual chicken festival that will make you question everything you thought you knew about poultry-based entertainment.

If you came here by accident, thinking you were headed to London, England, congratulations! You've just earned yourself a free lesson in regional geography and disappointment. But while you're here, why not embrace the quirks of this small-town treasure trove of Southern hospitality, questionable road infrastructure, and a steadfast commitment to deep-frying everything in sight?

Which brings us to our next killer. If you've ever complained about overachievers at work, allow me to introduce you to Donald Harvey—a man who took the phrase "going above and beyond" to truly horrifying levels. Known as the Angel of Death, Harvey was a mild-mannered hospital orderly by day, and a prolific serial killer... also by day—and sometimes night, depending on the shift schedule.

Unlike your average murder enthusiast, Harvey wasn't roaming the streets in a ski mask or carving cryptic messages into cornfields. No, he had the professionalism and time management skills to rack up an estimated thirty-seven

to fifty-seven kills while on the clock, because why commit crimes in your free time when you can multitask?

Born in 1952 in Butler County, Ohio, young Donald Harvey was the kind of child who makes you want to ask, "Where were the warning signs and why did everyone ignore them?" The short answer: everywhere and because it was the 1950s.

- Bullied at school? Check.
- Had a weird obsession with power and control? Naturally.
- Possibly suffered head trauma? Oh, of course. All the greats do.
- Developed an early fascination with death? Ding, ding, ding!

By the time he dropped out of high school (who needs an education when you have ambition?), he was well on his way to becoming the gold medalist in medical murder.

Some people enter the medical field to save lives. Others, like Harvey, enter it to quietly erase them while collecting a paycheck. He began his reign of terror in 1970 at Marymount Hospital in Kentucky, where he quickly realized that being an orderly came with an alarming lack of oversight.

Harvey discovered his talent for casual killing while tending to terminally ill patients, which is kind of like finding out you're really good at knitting, except with cyanide and morphine instead of yarn. He claimed his first murders were mercy killings, but much like a cat that "accidentally" knocks over your coffee, his definitions of accidental and intentional were questionable at best.

From there, it became a murder buffet:

- Arsenic? Classic.
- Cyanide? A timeless favorite.
- Suffocation with a pillow? Simple yet effective.
- Messing with people's oxygen tanks? Creative, but also very rude.

By the time anyone noticed the ridiculous uptick in "natural" deaths, Harvey had already moved from hospital to hospital, killing patients like he was some kind of macabre traveling salesman of doom.

You might be asking, "Why did no one stop him?" Well, welcome to American healthcare in the 1970s and '80s, where background checks were optional, and the phrase "patient mortality rates" was apparently just a suggestion.

At one point, a fellow nurse noticed Harvey rubbing feces into a patient's food, and instead of calling the police like a normal person, she just kind of ignored it. Because, you know, sometimes people have "quirks."

Red flags were flapping in hurricane-force winds yet nobody did a damn thing. Harvey even got caught stealing body parts from the morgue at one hospital, but instead of getting arrested, he was just asked to resign politely.

Serial killers dream of this level of job security.

Like all good things (and bad serial killers), Harvey's career had to come to an end. In 1987, the suspicious death of a patient led authorities to perform an autopsy (because, *finally*, someone decided to do their job). What did they find? Oh, just enough arsenic to kill an entire Thanksgiving dinner party.

When police raided his home, they found a serial killer's shopping list:

- Arsenic and cyanide? Stocked like a doomsday prepper.
- Medical books on poisoning? Casual light reading.
- A diary detailing his murders? Because why not keep records?

Faced with mountains of evidence and the world's most awkward sentencing hearing, Harvey claimed to have killed to over thirty-seven patients (though some estimate the

number could be much higher). He was sentenced to multiple life terms—because, unfortunately, the death penalty isn't retroactive.

While in London, you'd be remiss not to visit Finley's Fun Center, where it isn't just roller skating. It seriously isn't. It also features arcade games, laser tag, and a bounce house. We know you like those.

LEXINGTON, KENTUCKY

Robert Smallwood
Kills: 3
Span of Activity: 1993 to April 2006

Fun Fact: His sister, Elizabeth, was the eighth murder victim of the Edgecombe County Killer

Lexington, Kentucky—a city that lives, breathes, and probably bleeds thoroughbred racing. If you've ever wanted to experience what it feels like to be an extra in a Hallmark movie but with more bourbon and fewer realistic career opportunities, this is the place for you.

Known as the Horse Capital of the World, Lexington is the kind of town where people will casually drop the price of their latest foal into conversation ("Oh him? Just a three-million-dollar baby"), and you'll stand there, clutching your gas station coffee, wondering where it all went wrong.

No visit to Lexington is complete without faking enthusiasm for horse racing. Don't understand horse racing? No problem! Just yell things like, "Come on, Number 5!" and "I should've bet the trifecta!" and you'll fit right in. Keeneland is a place where men wear pastel suits unironically and women treat giant hats like a competitive sport. The crowd consists of actual wealthy horse breeders, the University of Kentucky students day-drinking at ten a.m., and at least one person who just lost their mortgage on a horse named Biscuit Boy.

Lexington is at the heart of the Bourbon Trail, which is basically Burning Man for people who prefer their souvenirs to come in 120-proof-filled glass bottles. You'll visit distilleries with names that sound like forgotten Civil War generals (Woodford

Reserve, Buffalo Trace, Four Roses) and each tour guide will remind you of the myth that bourbon must be made in Kentucky to be "real bourbon," as if this is the most sacred rule of civilization. You'll leave with a mild buzz, a newfound appreciation for charred oak barrels, and a deep concern about how much bourbon your tour guide actually drinks per shift.

Of course, you'll need the Local Culture Starter Pack!

- Own at least one piece of clothing with a UK Wildcats logo on it (mandatory, even for babies).
- Talk about bourbon like a sommelier, even if you secretly just mix it with Diet Coke.
- Have a strong opinion on horse racing, even if you don't watch it.
- Think Louisville is overrated and Cincinnati is practically Siberia.
- Consider "reckon so" a perfectly acceptable response in any conversation.

No trip to Lexington would be complete if one didn't visit Robert Smallwood's old stomping grounds.

In the annals of criminal notoriety, Robert Smallwood Jr. stands out—not for his cunning or complexity, but for his unsettlingly mundane existence that masked a series of brutal crimes. Born in December 1973 in Lexington, Kentucky, Smallwood's life trajectory seemed unremarkable, making his descent into violence all the more jarring.

Smallwood's early years were devoid of the typical red flags we've come to expect from future felons. He married in 1997 and fathered five children, presenting the facade of a family man. However, beneath this veneer lay a propensity for violence that would soon surface.

In 1993, Smallwood committed his first known violent act by assaulting and raping eighty-three-year-old Viola Green in her home. Green survived the attack but passed away five years later, never seeing justice served. This incident marked the beginning of a series of assaults and murders that would plague Lexington for over a decade.

Smallwood's subsequent crimes followed a disturbing pattern:

- December 1999: He strangled a woman with her own clothing in her apartment.
- August 2002: He murdered a mother of six, leaving her body in a parking lot with signs of sexual assault.
- April 2006: He bound and strangled in her home, a crime that would eventually lead to his downfall.

For years, these murders were investigated in isolation, with no apparent connection. It wasn't until August 2006 that DNA evidence linked the crimes, revealing the presence of a serial killer in Lexington—a revelation that sent shockwaves through the community. Smallwood, already incarcerated for violating his parole on unrelated charges, was identified as the perpetrator through DNA matching.

Faced with overwhelming evidence, Smallwood pleaded guilty to the murders and was sentenced to life imprisonment without the possibility of parole in 2007. His case serves as a grim reminder of the potential for darkness lurking behind even the most unassuming facades.

While in Lexington, make sure you stop by the Chevy Chase Inn at 833 Euclid Ave. You may not be safe from serial killers there, but at least you can get an old-school drink.

OSAGE, WEST VIRGINIA

Eugene Blake
Kills: 3
Span of Activity: January 1967 to
October 1984

Fun Fact: Before he was paroled (only to murder again), Blake was known as a model prisoner

Nestled along the banks of the Monongahela River, Osage, West Virginia, is the kind of place you only find yourself in by accident or as part of some elaborate witness relocation program. It is a town where directions are given in relation to where things used to be—"Turn left at the old post office, which burned down in '87, and then right where the Dairy Queen almost opened but didn't."

If you're flying in, congratulations. You've made a terrible mistake. The nearest airport is in Pittsburgh, about ninety miles north, and from there, you'll need to rent a car, which may or may not survive the potholes that West Virginia's road maintenance team (one guy named Kenny) has declared part of the state's "natural charm." Should you arrive by train, you are either a Victorian ghost or someone whose GPS has betrayed them.

Eugene Blake was not the kind of man you want at your dinner party. He was not, for instance, the sort of guest who would bring a decent bottle of wine or politely pretend to enjoy your overcooked salmon. No, Blake was what some might call "socially inept," others "deeply disturbed," and his parole officer "a walking legal disaster."

Born in 1945, a time when people still thought lead paint was a fun snack for toddlers, Eugene Blake hailed from the kind of small-town America that specialized in churning out either high school football coaches or men who keep body parts in

their refrigerators. Unfortunately, Blake fell into the latter category.

Guilty of murdering three people, Blake had a knack for making friends, just not for very long. His first victim, an eighteen-year-old woman, was simply driving on West Virginia Route 75 when Blake ran her off the road, demanded money, and repeatedly stabbed her. She survived the initial stabbing but later died before arriving at the Cabell Huntington Hospital. Blake evaded a couple of angry vigilantes but was later caught, convicted, imprisoned, and commuted. Virginia is for lovers, and West Virginia is for Serial Killers.

After the governor commuted his sentence, Blake violated his parole by moving to Ohio for a bit, murdering a man and raping his girlfriend. Blake eluded capture and moved back to West Virginia, where he murdered another young girl. He was convicted and sentenced to life.

Many years later, investigators in Ohio finally linked the murder in Ohio to Blake due to semen left at the scene. To avoid the death sentence, he pleaded guilty to all charges and was sentenced to life imprisonment.... again.

Osage, West Virginia, isn't for the faint of heart, the weak of stomach, or the person expecting a quaint Appalachian getaway with scenic views and artisanal coffee. But if you're looking for something real—something unpolished and unapologetically itself—you just might find it here. Or at the very least, you'll find yourself wondering how soon you can leave. Before you do, check out the nearby Monongahela National Forest featuring more than 920,000 acres of flowers, trees, rivers, and lots of trails with no one else around. Maybe.

ALEXANDRIA, VIRGINIA

Montie Rissell
Kills: 5
Span of Activity: August 1976 to
May 1977

Fun Fact: Rissell was featured in Season 1, Episode 4 of the 2017 Netflix crime drama **Mindhunter**

Alexandria, Virginia—a city so charming it could make even a DMV employee crack a smile. Nestled just outside DC, this historic gem is best known for cobblestone streets, overpriced artisanal soaps, and its uncanny ability to make you feel underdressed no matter what you're wearing.

Stroll down King Street, where every building is so charming, you'll feel obligated to start speaking in ye olde English. Pop into one of the many boutique shops selling scented candles that cost as much as a minor surgery. Be sure to stop by the waterfront, where you can watch confused tourists board a water taxi they didn't mean to book.

If you enjoy history, expensive brunches, and pretending not to mind that you just paid seventeen bucks for a latte, Alexandria is a perfect mix of colonial charm and modern pretension, and by the end of your trip, you'll either be looking up real estate prices or aggressively Googling "cheaper places to live near DC." Either way, you'll leave with at least one overpriced souvenir and a lingering sense of financial insecurity.

Some men are born bad. Some are made that way. And some, like Montie Rissell, simply slide into the abyss without so much as a struggle—like a bloated corpse sinking into the Potomac, swallowed whole by the River of American Madness.

Rissell was not a household name like Bundy or Dahmer, but his crimes were no less grotesque, no less fueled by that same

seething cocktail of boredom, resentment, and cheap-motel-room depravity that breeds the worst of our species. A serial killer of convenience, one who did not stalk so much as seize, like a vulture waiting for roadkill.

Born in 1958 in Wellington, Kansas, Rissell came of age in the post-war haze of American normalcy—a world of neat lawns, trimmed hedges, and the unspoken horrors of suburbia. When his parents split, he moved with his mother to Virginia, that Southern-tinged land of Civil War ghosts and overpriced seafood joints. By all accounts, he was just another angsty kid with a lousy stepfather and a burgeoning grudge against the world.

Then came the first crack in the windshield. A petty criminal from the jump, Rissell started with the usual warm-up acts—breaking and entering, stealing cars, the kind of crimes that get you sent to juvenile detention, not death row. He was arrested for rape at fifteen, but the system, that great lumbering beast of blind justice, did what it does best.

It let him go.

By the time he was eighteen, Rissell had escalated from an amateur pervert to a full-blown predator. Between 1976 and 1977, he murdered five women he either knew or abducted at random. In Alexandria, Virginia, he didn't have the dramatic flourishes of a Zodiac or the media savvy of a Son of Sam; he wasn't writing taunting letters or carving symbols into corpses. No, Rissell was the kind of killer who lurks in the margins of a newspaper—the kind the FBI profiles with cold detachment.

His victims? Women who crossed his path at the wrong time. His method? Rape and murder, carried out with the same eerie nonchalance as a man taking out the trash. He would later claim that he murdered because his victims "talked too much," a statement so callous it reads like the punchline to a bad joke told in a gas station at three a.m.

And yet, Rissell wasn't stupid. When he was finally caught, he cooperated with law enforcement like a man who knew the game was up. He didn't resist, didn't throw a theatrical fit in the courtroom. He simply confessed, laid it all out with the mechanical precision of a man detailing his grocery list.

Sentenced to life in prison, Rissell vanished from the public eye, one more beast caged in the American penal system. He wasn't a media darling like Charles Manson or a cautionary tale like Jeffrey Dahmer. There were no bestselling books about him, no Hollywood adaptations. He was a footnote, a whisper, a reminder that sometimes the real monsters don't wear masks—they walk among us, unnoticed, until it's too late.

In prison, Rissell reportedly showed a high IQ and even assisted in psychological studies about serial killers, but what good is intelligence when it's wasted on the irredeemable? He was just another case file, another name in the long, unending parade of human rot that litters the annals of crime history.

Now, if you're looking for a true dive bar, you're going to have to lower your standards (and probably head further south). But The Birchmere kind of counts—mostly because it has sticky floors, a bar, and regular performances by musicians whose heyday was three decades ago. Go here if you want to say, "I saw that guy who used to be in a band you vaguely remember."

RICHMOND, VIRGINIA

Timothy Wilson Spencer—aka the Southside Strangler
Kills: 5
Span of Activity: September 1984 to November 1988

Let's head south to Virginia, where Virginia was for lovers but is now for psychopathic killers.

Richmond, Virginia, is filled with cobblestone streets, Civil War ghosts, and a burgeoning class of hipster barons slinging cold brew and overpriced records. It's the South, but not *The South*. A place where rebel flags and BLM murals exist on the same cracked city block. The air hums with revolution, fueled by cheap beer, broken dreams, and a perverse dedication to historic preservation.

Forget the hotels—sterile monstrosities where businessmen sip bad coffee and pretend they aren't in Hell. Find a questionable Airbnb in Church Hill, preferably in a house that looks like it has seen at least one violent exorcism. You want character, not comfort. Bonus points if it's haunted.

Richmond is a city that exists on the brink—of history, of culture, of complete and utter chaos. It is beautiful in the way that abandoned amusement parks and old typewriters are beautiful: haunted, weird, and brimming with stories you'll never quite understand.

Timothy Wilson Spencer is a name that slithered through Richmond like a sewer rat, whispering horror in the ears of anyone paying attention. He wasn't a celebrity. He wasn't a mastermind. No, Spencer was something worse: an efficient, invisible nightmare who skulked the edges of the 1980s,

preying on women with the kind of clinical precision that makes the skin crawl.

Spencer was a Richmond native, a product of a world where hope was just another empty promise. Born in 1962, he grew up in a city where the past and present fought like drunken bar brawlers, leaving little room for a future. His childhood? Uneventful, forgettable—no early warning signs that he'd grow into a monster, no fireworks of youthful depravity. Just another kid lost in the shuffle.

Between 1987 and 1988, he earned his moniker, the Southside Strangler. His method was disturbingly precise. He stalked, he waited, he struck. He used ligatures, controlled the crime scenes, left behind nothing but terror and the faint echo of his own depravity. Women in Richmond and around Arlington lived in fear, the shadow of a faceless predator growing longer with every victim.

Spencer was a pioneer in the worst way possible. The first man in US history convicted by DNA evidence, science cornered him where the police had failed; his arrogance, his belief in his own invisibility, shattered by the hard truth of forensic biology. It was the twentieth century catching up to the monster, pinning him like an insect under a microscope.

In 1994, the Commonwealth of Virginia sent him to the electric chair. He died the way he lived—silent, unremarkable, a blip in the collective consciousness of true crime. No rambling last words, just a nod before the hood covered his head, the dull hum of justice grinding him into dust.

He did leave his mark in the history books though. His DNA conviction set the precedent for a new age of forensic justice, a warning to killers who believed they were untouchable.

No Richmond experience is complete without getting absolutely wrecked in a bar that smells like despair and victory.

Enter Cobra Cabana—a tattoo-required, punk-rock bar in the heart of Carver. The neon beer signs flicker like they might explode at any moment. The bartenders look like they've been up for three days straight, and the clientele consists of washed-up musicians, nihilistic art students, and at least one guy who swears he saw Bigfoot in the woods outside Ashland. The drinks are strong, the music is loud, and the likelihood of an impromptu mosh pit is disturbingly high. Order a Cobra Burger and a shot of whatever whiskey won't make you blind. Stay long enough and you'll either make a lifelong friend or a permanent enemy.

ALEXANDRIA, VIRGINIA

Charles Severance—aka the Grudge Killer
Kills: 3
Span of Activity: December 2003 to February 2014

Fun Fact: He ran for mayor of Alexandria and Congress

Let's travel back to Alexandria, Virginia.

First, you'll need to cross the Hellscape that is the DC metro area. If you survive the Beltway traffic without flipping off a diplomat or driving straight into the Potomac, congratulations—you're already a warrior. Just take I-95 South but be prepared to question every life decision as you sit in an endless sea of brake lights and existential dread. Pro tip: an emergency flask is essential. The Founding Fathers would approve.

Alexandria, Virginia—a town so steeped in American history that even the ghosts are probably over it. Cobblestone streets, charming colonial homes, and overpriced boutiques so aggressively quaint they might as well slap you with a tricorn hat on arrival. This isn't just a city. It's where the past refuses to die, clutching its powdered wig and whispering, "We fought the British for this?"

Old Town Alexandria is the beating heart of this place. Picture it: a group of lobbyists, having chi lattes at a sidewalk café with congressional pages while juggling three smartphones—one for work, one for personal use, and a burner for the important people. George Washington probably bought moonshine here, but now it's all "locally sourced kombucha" and "organic kale chips."

Walk the waterfront along the Potomac River, where street performers juggle and tourists snap selfies with overpriced ice cream cones. Or dive into history at the Torpedo Factory Art Center, a former munitions plant now filled with starving artists silently judging your lack of taste.

If you're the sentimental type, visit Christ Church, where Washington and Robert E. Lee once prayed. Imagine the ghosts of American history silently screaming, "It was all for THIS?!"

Some men are born strange; others are made that way—but Charles Severance? He came into this world with a crooked grin and chaos stitched into his DNA, the kind of man who could sip a cup of coffee in the morning and still hear the static of demons whispering in his ear by nightfall.

Born in 1960, Severance seemed like just another cog in America's ever-churning machine. He attended the University of Virginia; yes, that proud institution where young minds bloom, though it's unclear whether Severance was there to absorb knowledge or simply marinate in the darker corners of academia. He eventually earned a degree in mechanical engineering, though it's anyone's guess if he was more interested in machinery or in the twisted gears spinning inside his own skull.

In 1996 and again in 2000, this ghoul-in-waiting ran for mayor and congress. He was a scraggly figure spouting paranoid ramblings about elitists, the "oppressors," and the decaying moral core of the city. His campaign slogans read more like apocalyptic prophecies scrawled on a gas station bathroom wall.

But Severance wasn't just another failed political clown. No, there was something murkier festering beneath that wild beard and vacant stare.

Severance, after a plane torpedoed into the Pentagon, changed his life's mission from running a modern-day Sodom to randomly murdering people as they answered their door. "Knock. Talk. Enter. Kill. Exit. Murder" is what Severance called it.

Between 2003 and 2014, Alexandria—a place already haunted by history—became the hunting ground for Severance's madness. His victims were symbols of the world he'd come to hate: affluent, respected, and living in homes that embodied the privilege he despised.

Beginning in 2003, Severance gunned down Nancy Dunning, the wife of the county sheriff and a local real estate agent. She was a test run because all engineers must prove the hypothesis first. Severance rang her doorbell and fired, leaving her dead among the trappings of suburban comfort.

In 2013, he killed Ron Kirby, a transportation planner, a man who dedicated his life to improving the city Severance so deeply resented. He too was gunned down at his front door. The irony of planning the city's routes while being trapped in Severance's own deranged path was brutal. In 2014, beloved music teacher Ruthanne Lodato opened her front door one morning to what she thought was an ordinary visitor. Severance shot her point blank in the chest, an act so cold and methodical it felt almost surgical.

This wasn't random. This was a manifesto in bullets, a twisted crusade against what he saw as the corrupt elite. Severance believed these "doorway murders" were a form of social justice, some deranged purge against those he thought had poisoned society. The door was his symbol—the barrier between the haves and the have-nots, and he obliterated it with a pull of the trigger.

When they finally caught him in 2014, he was living in his car, spiraling deeper into paranoia. The trial was a carnival of

madness, filled with rambling statements about conspiracies, mind control, and societal decay. But even as the gavel dropped, there was an undeniable sense that Charles Severance wasn't the only madman—he was a symptom of something uglier festering beneath the surface of America's glossy, historic facades.

Now he rots in a cell, his twisted crusade silenced, but the echoes of his madness still linger, proof that even in places as polished as Alexandria, the darkness is only a doorbell away.

While in Alexandria, forget your artisanal cocktails and wine bars where people use "mouthfeel" unironically. You need grit. You need The Light Horse. A dive bar masquerading as a sports bar, it sits on King Street like a hangover you can't shake. Upstairs, it's all candle-lit charm and overpriced whiskey. But downstairs—oh, that's where the magic happens.

Dim lights. Sticky floors. A jukebox that hasn't been updated since the H.W. Bush administration. This is where the off-duty waitstaff and jaded locals come to drink cheap beer and air their existential grievances. Order a PBR and a shot of rail whiskey. Play a round of darts, but only if you're feeling lucky—or nihilistic.

ROCKY MOUNT, NORTH CAROLINA

Edgecombe County Serial Killer
Kills: 10-11
Span of Activity: May 2005 to
March 2009

Edgecombe County, North Carolina, where a patch of Earth where tobacco ghosts still hauntingly roam the fields, barbecue smoke lingers like a stubborn memory, and the line between reality and madness blurs faster than your third shot of bottom-shelf vodka at a dusty dive off Highway 64.

Edgecombe isn't the glossy South you see in travel brochures. No, this is the raw, unfiltered underbelly—where the rivers run slow, the heat bakes your skull, and the people talk like they've got secrets they'll take to the grave.

The Edgecombe County Killer is a phantom prowling in the shadows of North Carolina's underbelly, a specter born from the swamps and backroads where the American dream goes to die.

The unidentified Edgecombe County serial killer used the surroundings of Edgecombe and Halifax counties in North Carolina as his playground. There are ten suspected victims, all African American women; the remains of eight have been recovered. Because some of the victims had been found near the Seven Bridges Road in Rocky Mount, the culprit has also been called the Seven Bridges Killer. All the victims were engaged in sex work and had problems with drug addiction at various times.

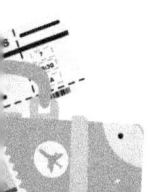

Every town worth its salt has a dive bar. A place where dreams come to drown and the beer's always cold enough to make you forget your regrets.

In Edgecombe County, that place is Melanie's Place, an unassuming shack with a neon sign that flickers like it's got PTSD. Located just outside Tarboro near a forgotten bend in the river, it's the kind of joint where the jukebox still plays Johnny Cash, the bartender calls you "hon" whether you like it or not, and the regulars eye you like you just kicked their dog.

Inside, it's a haze of cigarette smoke, dollar bills tacked to the ceiling, and stories that range from the mundane to the downright insane. I met a man there named Billy Ray who swore he saw Bigfoot back in '97. Bought me a beer just to tell the tale—that's Southern hospitality for you.

FAYETTEVILLE, NORTH CAROLINA

Ronald Gray
Kills: 4
Span of Activity: April 1986 to January 1987

Welcome to Fayetteville, North Carolina, where the humidity slaps you like an angry drill sergeant, and the bars serve up the booze with a side of existential dread. If you're here, it's probably because you got stationed at Fort Bragg, lost a bet, or have an inexplicable fondness for strip-mall culture. Either way, buckle up, because you're in for a wild ride.

Fort Bragg is the beating, boot-stomping heart of this town, home to the 82nd Airborne Division, Special Forces, and more testosterone than a bullfight in Mexico City. This place is the Pentagon's favorite war machine, where elite soldiers jump out of planes for fun and eat MREs like they're gourmet meals.

Tourists? You better have a reason to be here—preferably in the form of a military ID or an invitation from a grizzled vet who has a story about being shot at in three different countries. If you're lucky, you might catch a training exercise where men in camo rappel out of helicopters like heavily armed Tarzans. If you're unlucky, you'll accidentally wander into an off-limits zone and find yourself surrounded by very serious men with very large rifles.

If you make it inside, be sure to check out the 82nd Airborne Division War Memorial Museum—a shrine to paratroopers who've leapt into every major American conflict since WWII. If that doesn't make you crave a stiff drink, nothing will.

After Fort Bragg, you'll want to head to Hay Street, the neon-lit artery of downtown where military paychecks vanish faster than a bottle of Jack in a barracks room. It's a mix of tattoo parlors, dive bars, and regret-fueled spending sprees, with a few decent spots for food if you need to soak up the damage.

If you want to eat something that won't give you bad memories, try Circa 1800—a solid spot with Southern food that's fancy enough to impress a date but still serves moonshine cocktails strong enough to knock out a mid-level officer.

For something more... questionable, head to one of the 24-hour gas stations and order whatever's been spinning under a heat lamp since sunrise. The risk of food poisoning merely adds to the thrill.

Born in 1965, Ronald A. Gray grew up in Indiana, a place where cornfields stretch out like the dull flatlines of forgotten America. He joined the United States Army, found his way to Fort Bragg, and seemed to settle into the structured life of a military man. But beneath the uniform, something festered. A predator.

Between 1986 and 1987, Gray unleashed a brutal rampage of murder and rape on the unsuspecting streets surrounding Fort Bragg. He didn't bother with complex motives or deep psychological rationalizations. This was about power, control, and a sickening bloodlust that made him one of the most terrifying figures to ever wear US Army fatigues.

He stalked women—military and civilian alike. He raped them, tortured them, and killed them, disposing of their bodies like discarded beer cans. The crimes were vicious, the kind that sends chills down the spines of even the most hardened detectives. Four dead, multiple assaults, and an entire military town gripped in terror.

JOHNNY TREVISANI with BRIAN WHITNEY

You can only hide a killing spree for so long when you live on a military base. Gray wasn't a genius. He wasn't some Hannibal Lecter-level mastermind playing cat and mouse with the authorities. He was a brute—a reckless, violent opportunist who thought the Army would protect him.

But even Fort Bragg had its limits. When investigators started piecing together the pattern—the attacks, the evidence, the horror stories from survivors who barely escaped—Gray's number was up. His arrest wasn't dramatic. No blaze of glory. No last stand. Just a killer caught in his own web of depravity.

The Army court-martial didn't hesitate. They saw what he was: a disgrace, a beast in uniform. He was sentenced to death in 1988. The civilian courts didn't go easy on him either. He collected multiple life sentences from North Carolina for his crimes outside the base.

Still, the wheels of justice turn slow, and the US military hasn't executed a soldier since 1961. So Gray sits on death row, locked away in the bowels of Fort Leavenworth, rotting like the human filth he is, appealing his sentence, playing the long game, hoping to outlast the system.

For decades, Ronald Gray remained a shadow—a living ghost in the military's prison system, a reminder that even the most disciplined institutions breed monsters. His death warrant was signed multiple times, once by President George W. Bush in 2008, and then challenged in the courts as death penalty debates raged.

But no amounts of appeals, legal loopholes, no bureaucratic stalling could erase what he did. In a world obsessed with serial killers, with Netflix specials and true crime podcasts turning butchers into celebrities, Gray never became infamous—just reviled. No one tells his story for entertainment. His crimes weren't stylish, his motives weren't twisted puzzles for amateur sleuths to unravel. He was a predator in uniform, a stain on the Army, a walking nightmare who left bodies in his wake.

You haven't really experienced Fayetteville until you've stumbled into a dive bar and The Doghouse is the kind of establishment that makes even hardened veterans reconsider their life choices.

This place is dimly lit, sticky-floored, and filled with people who look like they either just got back from a deployment or just got out of jail. The beer is cheap, the jukebox is loud, and the bartenders have seen things that would make a CIA operative break down in tears.

The signature drink? The "Bragg Special"—which, depending on the bartender, is either a tall glass of gin or something neon-colored that tastes like an energy drink having an identity crisis.

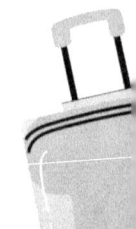

BARNWELL, SOUTH CAROLINA

Henry Louis Wallace—aka the Taco Bell Strangler
Kills: 11
Span of Activity: March 1990 to March 1994

Fun Fact: Wallace attended some of his victims' funerals and even comforted their families

The road into Barnwell, South Carolina, is long, flat, and lined with the kind of pine trees that stand like silent witnesses to backwoods deals gone sideways. This is the Deep South—where the air is thick, the sweet tea is practically syrup, and people give you a slow, knowing nod before deciding whether they like you or not.

Barnwell isn't a town you just stumble into; it's a town you end up in either by fate or by running out of gas. Founded in 1785, Barnwell has the quiet charm of a place that could either lull you into nostalgia or make you feel like you've stepped into a Faulkner novel, where something sinister is always lurking just below the surface. It's got the usual suspects: a courthouse that looks like it knows things, a downtown strip that's seen better days, and a handful of churches making sure everyone stays mostly on the straight and narrow.

Barnwell isn't for the faint of heart. It's for the traveler who can appreciate the poetry of a one-light town, the beauty of a conversation with an old-timer at a gas station, and the quiet thrill of knowing you've found a place that most people will never bother to stop for.

Come for the history. Stay for the beer. Leave before the ghosts find you.

Henry Louis Wallace was born on November 4, 1965, in Barnwell, South Carolina. A town so small and inconsequential

that even the ghosts get bored. His mother, a strict, God-fearing woman, ran the house like a boot camp. There was no father in the picture, no comfort, no warmth—just the slow, creeping realization that the world was an unforgiving place.

People who knew Wallace as a child said he was quiet but polite, well mannered, and softspoken—all the classic markers of a boy who had already learned to hide what was inside. He made it through high school, ran track, joined clubs, and put on the mask of an average kid.

But underneath, the rot had already set in.

After high school, Wallace bounced through life like a drifter with a résumé, attending college sporadically before enlisting in the Navy in 1985. He served as a communications specialist—which sounds important, but really just meant he knew how to keep secrets.

Then came the small crimes, the warning signs, the early tremors of something darker. Wallace started stealing, getting arrested for shoplifting in 1988. If life had any kind of justice, this would have been the moment someone looked closer. But in America, if you wear the right smile and say the right things, you can walk past every alarm bell without so much as a glance.

In the early 1990s, Wallace moved to Charlotte, North Carolina—a city growing fast, its skyline stretching upward while its underbelly remained as dark and hungry as ever. Here, Wallace found the perfect hunting ground.

From 1992 to 1994, Henry Louis Wallace wove his way through Charlotte like a ghost, preying on young Black women, most of them people he knew—friends, coworkers, women who trusted him just enough to let him inside. That was all he needed. It was during this period that he became a manager at a Taco Bell at the now defunct Eastland Mall. A fact that most people at Taco Bell want customers to "think outside the bun(dy)."

His method was calculated but casual, the way a man flicks a cigarette into the gutter without thinking about where it lands. He didn't storm in like some masked slasher—he used charm, familiarity, and patience. He knew his victims' routines, their weaknesses; he had their trust.

He would talk his way into their homes, tie them up, strangle them, and sometimes assault them before staging their bodies like grotesque afterthoughts. Then, with a predator's ease, he would return to normal life: showing up to work, laughing with friends, even attending some of his victims' funerals like an actor trapped in the sickest role imaginable.

For two years, the city didn't see it coming.

This wasn't a white-gloved suburban nightmare where police rush to find the missing cheerleader. No, these were young Black women, working-class, often overlooked, their disappearances and murders stacking up like some awful, unspoken epidemic.

The police didn't connect the dots fast enough. The press barely whispered about it. And Wallace? Wallace just kept slithering in the shadows, a specter in human form.

By early 1994, Charlotte had a full-blown serial killer problem, though the city still hadn't caught on. But every predator makes mistakes and Wallace was no exception. His final murders, including the brutal killing of eighteen-year-old Brandi Henderson, left behind too much evidence, too many threads leading back to the same man.

On March 13, 1994, police finally arrested Henry Louis Wallace.

The trial was a Southern spectacle—televised, dramatized, the whole town watching as Wallace finally stood before the Court. His defense tried to sell him as a victim of abuse, a man whose mind had been warped by a cruel upbringing, but there was no sympathy left to buy.

In 1997, Wallace was sentenced to death.

And yet—he's still alive.

Decades later, Wallace sits in Central Prison in Raleigh, North Carolina, his execution date continuously delayed, his existence reduced to a long, slow wait in a cell. Ten women dead, a city haunted, and yet the so-called Taco Bell Strangler still breathes.

Before you leave Barnwell, check out King George Lavender, which features over one hundred acres of eight thousand lavender plants in large, rolling fields. Whether you're looking to have a big event like getting married, want a lovely horse-drawn carriage ride, or you're looking for a place to lie down on your back, look at the sky, and smoke a ton of weed (discreetly: NC is still not a legal state), this is the place for you.

LITTLE ROCK, ARKANSAS

Little Rock Serial Killer—aka the Little Rock Slasher
Kills: 3
Span of Activity: August 2020 to April 2021

Little Rock, Arkansas—the name alone sounds like a bad omen, like a place you end up rather than a place you go. But don't let that fool you. This is the true South, a strange cocktail of backwoods grit and modern ambition, where politics, whiskey, and ghosts all share the same block.

This is Clinton Country, a place where everyone has a story about the time they met Bill, and where the past still lingers like the smell of BBQ smoke at dawn. It's a city that's too big to be a small town but too small to be a real city—a weird, liminal space where history and progress are in a slow-motion fistfight.

If you come here looking for a good time, you'll find it. If you come looking for trouble, you'll find that too.

Between August 2020 and April 2021, an unseen predator emerged—a figure as elusive as a shadow in the dark, christened by the media as the "Little Rock Slasher." This specter haunted the city's streets, leaving a trail of blood and unanswered questions, then vanished as mysteriously as he appeared.

The Slasher's campaign began on August 24, 2020, with the brutal stabbing of sixty-four-year-old Larry Eugene McChristian. Found lifeless on a stranger's porch at 2200 South Gaines Street, Larry's murder baffled authorities. Surveillance footage revealed a chilling scene: the assailant

approached Larry, stabbed him, walked away, then returned to inflict further wounds before disappearing into the night.

A month later, on September 23, sixty-two-year-old Jeff Welch was discovered dead on his front porch at 4128 West 12th Street, a puncture wound in his neck. Initially deemed suspicious, an autopsy confirmed it as homicide, linking it to the previous killing.

After a six-month lull, the Slasher struck again. On April 11, 2021, forty-one-year-old Debra Walker was viciously attacked near 1906 South Pulaski Street, suffering fifteen stab wounds. Miraculously, she survived and provided a description: a slender, over six-foot-tall Black male. Less than twenty-four hours later, forty-year-old Marlon Anthony Franklin was found stabbed to death at 2710 Wright Avenue, a block from Walker's attack site.

After April 2021, the Slasher's knife fell silent. No further attacks were reported, leaving the city in a state of uneasy relief. Had he moved on, been incarcerated for unrelated crimes, or met his own demise? The questions lingered, but answers remained elusive.

The Little Rock Slasher's tale is one of fear, mystery, and the unknown lurking within urban shadows. His identity remains a cipher, his motives inscrutable. As time marches on, the memory of his reign fades, but the scars he left on the city endure—a chilling reminder of the darkness that can dwell among us, unseen and unbidden.

After you're done walking the streets of the killing grounds, stop by Midtown Billiards (1316 South Main Street, Little Rock). This place is legendary for one reason: it only gets better after midnight.

This is a true after-hours bar, which means when every other bar closes, Midtown keeps the party going until the sun comes up. It's the kind of place where the drinks are stiff, the pool tables are always occupied, and the crowd is a perfect mix of service industry workers, bikers, college kids, and lost souls who need "just one more drink." The vibe is dark, loud, and slightly dangerous—but in a fun way. They are friendly with the strong drinks and their midtown burger is also famous for saving lives at three a.m.

MEMPHIS, TENNESSEE

South Memphis Killer
Kills: 3-4
Span of Activity: January 27 to February 26, 2011 (possibly September 2015)

Fun Fact: All the killer's victims were found in or near the same cemetery

Welcome to South Memphis—Where the Blues Bleed and the Barbecue Smokes Eternal

There are cities, then there are mythologies disguised as cities. Memphis is the latter.

It sits on the banks of the Mississippi like a battle-scarred old fighter—too stubborn to die, too proud to change. And if Memphis itself is the beast, then South Memphis is its beating, bloodied heart.

This is not the polished, tourist-friendly Memphis of Beale Street neon or Graceland fanatics taking selfies in their Elvis wigs. No, South Memphis is something older, rougher, realer. This is where the blues were born, where the ribs will make you cry, and where history drips from the walls like sweat on a July afternoon.

If you're looking for an easy, sanitized vacation, turn back now. But if you want to feel the pulse of Memphis in your chest like a bass drum at a juke joint at two a.m., then keep reading.

In the shadowed alleys and forgotten corners of South Memphis, a sinister rhythm took hold in early 2011. A dance of death that preyed upon the city's most vulnerable. Between January and February, the bodies of three women—Tamakia McKinney, Jessica Lewis, and Rhonda Wells—were discovered, each life extinguished by a faceless predator. A fourth victim,

Katrina Peterson, survived a brutal attack, her testimony painting a chilling portrait of a young man with cornrows driving a dark vehicle.

The city's underbelly trembled as these murders unfolded, casting a pall over the streets where the blues once thrived. The victims, all sex workers, were found discarded near Mt. Carmel Cemetery, a grim resting place that bore witness to their final moments. Despite the collection of DNA evidence and the release of a composite sketch, the assailant remained a ghost, slipping through the fingers of law enforcement and leaving a community in fear.

In September 2015, the specter of violence resurfaced with the murder of Juanita Gilmore, another sex worker found slain in a South Memphis cemetery. While the method differed—a stabbing rather than a shooting—the eerie similarities reignited fears of a serial killer stalking the streets. Yet, as years drifted by, these cases languished in the cold files, the killer's identity as elusive as the smoke wafting from Beale Street's juke joints. This dark chapter in Memphis's history remains unresolved, a haunting reminder of the lives lost and the justice that still eludes them.

Sure, everyone will tell you to visit Graceland, and sure, you could do that. But after walking the streets where a killer stalked their prey, I would recommend visiting the Stax Museum of American Soul Music. Because hearing where the birth of soul music began can be better than seeing where people's souls left the city.

GULFPORT, MISSISSIPPI

Donald Leroy Evans—The
Galveston Grifter
Kills: 3–70+
Span of Activity: March 1985 to
August 1991

Gulfport, Mississippi, is a city that shouldn't exist but does anyway.

This place has been drowned by hurricanes, rebuilt by hustlers, and haunted by the ghosts of bad decisions. It's where the deep-fried underbelly of the South meets the lawless humidity of the Gulf, and where every neon-lit dive bar is full of people who either just lost a fortune at the casino or just got out of county lockup.

It's a port town in every sense—a place of transit, where the salty air mixes with the sweat of men who work just hard enough to afford a long night of bourbon and questionable company.

If you come looking for tourist attractions, you'll find casinos, beaches, and some sanitized versions of Southern charm. But if you want to see the real Gulfport—the raw, unfiltered, heart of this place, then you need to go where the neon is flickering and the floors are tacky.

Every so often, America births a killer so absurdly evil, so detached from human life, that their very existence feels like a cruel practical joke from the cosmos. Donald Leroy Evans was one of those men.

He was a serial killer with no pattern, no motive, no logic. Just chaos wrapped in the skin of a man who could disappear as easily as he arrived.

By the time they caught him, he claimed to have killed more than seventy people. But Donald Leroy Evans was a liar. A pathological grifter who lived on deception and shadows. Evans was born in 1957, in Michigan, though he would later say whatever suited him about his early years.

There was no great childhood horror story, no dramatic trauma to pin his madness on—just a born predator, the kind of man who could smile and kill in the same breath.

By the 1970s, Evans was already on his way to nowhere. Petty crime, vagrancy, violence—his life was a road map of bad decisions and even worse impulses.

Prison didn't scare him. Work didn't interest him. Stability was a foreign concept.

Instead, he chose the life of a nomadic parasite—hitchhiking, panhandling, stealing, and killing when the mood struck.

Evans was the type of predator who thrived in the forgotten places of America. He targeted drifters, runaways, sex workers, and the unseen. The people no one bothered to look for until it was too late. His murders stretched across Mississippi, Florida, Georgia, Louisiana, Texas. The whole Gulf Coast, a killing field where he blended into the crowd like a shadow that never faded.

In 1991, he kidnapped and killed his last known victim. Ten-year-old Beatrice Louise Routh was abducted from Gulfport Park in Gulfport, Mississippi.

In the end, while in prison, Donald Leroy Evans was stabbed to death, his blood washing down the drain, forgotten even faster than the victims he pretended to not have killed.

Before you leave Gulfport, make sure you visit the famous the Julep Room (1217 Washington Avenue, Ocean Springs, Mississippi). The Julep Room is a basement speakeasy that's been serving drinks since the days when people still smuggled whiskey across state lines.

Elvis used to drink here. You can still feel him in the walls.

It's dimly lit, full of strange energy, and the kind of place where deals are made with a handshake and a lie.

Order a bourbon. Sit at the bar. Listen.

If you stay long enough, someone will tell you a story about a murder that never made the news.

MONTGOMERY, ALABAMA

Rhonda Belle Martin
Kills: 6
Span of Activity: 1937 to 1951

Montgomery is a city built on contradictions. The birthplace of the Civil Rights Movement, but also the former capital of the Confederacy. The streets still hum with the echoes of both. A city forever caught in the act of remembering and forgetting.

A place where history isn't just remembered. It lingers like cigarette smoke in an old man's car. The air is thick with ghosts—Civil Rights ghosts, Confederate ghosts, political ghosts whispering in the alleys, and some whiskey-soaked barflies who look like they might be ghosts but are just really, really drunk.

If you come here expecting a sanitized, theme-park version of Southern history, go back to Atlanta.

Montgomery is not polite, not polished, and not always pretty. But it is real, raw, and weird in all the right ways.

So grab a stiff drink, put on something that can handle high humidity and low expectations, and prepare for a trip through the capital of the American contradiction.

Rhonda Belle Martin, a killer in pearls, a homemaker with a lethal hobby. Martin was no violent slasher or bloodthirsty fiend. No, she was something far worse. She was a Southern mother with a gentle hand and a lethal touch, a woman who killed with patience and a smile, who kept feeding her victims until they were too weak to fight back.

This was not a crime of passion nor was it insanity. This was slow, methodical murder—an entire dynasty of death.

And like so many other horrors, it all happened in Alabama.

Rhonda Belle Martin was born in 1907 in the kind of quiet, unremarkable Southern town where no one asks too many questions and everyone minds their own business.

She was plain-looking, soft-spoken, the kind of woman you'd forget if you weren't married to her. And if you were married to her? Well, good luck surviving that.

By the time she reached adulthood, she had a taste for two things: marriage and murder. And over the years, she would mix them both in a deadly cocktail. She married six times. And somehow, five of those husbands mysteriously fell sick.

Between 1937 and 1951, Martin managed to kill six of her closest family members: five of her own children and one of her husbands. And to make things weirder, she poisoned two other husbands who somehow managed to survive.

This wasn't just a string of bad luck or a curse—this was systematic, slow-motion annihilation.

And through it all? She kept on cooking dinner like nothing was wrong.

In 1956, Rhonda Belle Martin was finally arrested. Although she initially confessed to all the murders she was accused of committing, she later recanted her confession in the murders of two of her children.

On October 11, 1957, in Alabama's Kilby Prison, Rhonda Belle Martin walked to the electric chair—a stark contrast to the quiet, slow deaths she had inflicted on her family.

As she sat down, there were no screams, no protests, no wild declarations of innocence.

Her final request?

A hamburger, mashed potatoes, cinnamon rolls, and coffee.

Simple. Plain. Like the life she pretended to lead.

They flipped the switch, and in a few short seconds, the black widow of Montgomery was no more. Martin's execution made her the third and final woman to be electrocuted in Alabama before the *Furman v. Georgia* ruling, as well as the last woman put to death in the state until 2002.

Before you move on from Montgomery, every town has a bar where the drinks are strong, the crowd is weird, and the night could go in any direction.

In Montgomery, that bar is The Exchange.

It's dark. The floors are questionably sticky. The bartender looks like he's seen some things and doesn't care about your life story. The people at the bar are a chaotic mix of gamblers, off-duty cops, confused tourists, and old guys who know something you don't.

Order a PBR. Sit down. Listen.

If someone starts telling you a conspiracy theory about Alabama politics, just nod along and buy them a drink. You might learn something.

ATLANTA, GEORGIA

Wayne Williams—aka the Atlanta Monster
Kills: 2-30
Span of Activity: July 21, 1979, to May 21, 1981

Fun Fact: Williams constructed his own carrier current radio station and dabbled in becoming a pop music producer and manager

The first thing you need to know about Atlanta is that it doesn't give a damn whether you're ready for it or not. The city sprawls like a drunken octopus, highways twisting in ways that make sense only to those born into the madness. It's a place where Southern hospitality meets an unrelenting grind, where the ghosts of the Civil War and the martyrs of the Civil Rights Movement haunt every street corner.

While there, seek refuge at The Majestic Diner on Ponce. It's been there since 1929, feeding the city's insomniacs, drunks, and philosophers with greasy-spoon classics and coffee strong enough to burn the lining of your stomach. At three a.m., it's a carnival of the damned—exhausted bartenders, aspiring rappers, wide-eyed college kids riding the comedown of a psychedelic trip.

Wayne Williams, for those unfamiliar, is the man widely believed to be responsible for the Atlanta Child Murders of 1979 to 1981, a period in which at least twenty-eight Black children, teenagers, and young adults disappeared or were found dead across the city. He was convicted for two of the killings, but authorities pinned many of the others on him, either officially or through a kind of exhausted shrugging, the way one might blame a missing sandwich on the office fridge thief even without proof.

Williams himself was something of an odd duck, the kind of man who probably corrected people about grammar at parties but had no friends to invite him to one. He was an aspiring music producer, which in the 1970s was code for "man with a tape recorder in his basement." He also dabbled in freelance photography, a hobby that, in retrospect, makes his entire existence more unsettling. No one wants their last known photo to be taken by an amateur with delusions of grandeur.

The way he got caught is the kind of detail that makes you wonder if fate was tired of him. The police had staked out Atlanta's bridges, believing the killer was dumping bodies into the Chattahoochee River. Sure enough, one night they heard a splash and pulled over a twenty-three-year-old Williams, who was driving a Chevy station wagon and sweating through his alibi. His excuse? He was on his way to audition a singer. At three a.m. Near a river.

Williams was sentenced to life imprisonment. Despite numerous attempts at appeals, he is still incarcerated.

By now, you may need a drink. You can seek the madness at the Clermont Lounge, the last true dive bar in a city obsessed with reinvention. This is where old strippers go to die—or keep dancing. You'll drink cheap beer under flickering neon, the stale scent of decades-old cigarette smoke clinging to your clothes. If you make the mistake of pulling out your phone to document the scene, a bouncer will materialize like a vengeful spirit to remind you that this is sacred ground. Be respectful, tip heavily, and don't ask too many questions.

NEW ORLEANS, LOUISIANA

The Storyville Slayer
Kills: 12+
Span of Activity: July 1991 to April 1996

New Orleans is not a city. It's a living, sweating, trumpet-blaring organism that thrives on excess and the questionable decisions of its visitors. You don't "see" New Orleans; you surrender to it. You let the humidity wrap around you like a damp, drunken hug from a stranger. You follow the scent of fried seafood and spilled beer down narrow streets that reek of history and sin.

For those in search of something truly bizarre, abandon Bourbon Street (a tourist trap designed to test the limits of human shame) and head to the Museum of Death. Yes, that's right. A whole museum dedicated to murder, funeral rituals, and crime scene photography. You'll see letters from serial killers, mortuary tools, and enough grotesque history to make you question why you ever thought a trip to New Orleans would be "fun." It's morbid, unsettling, and completely in line with the city's obsession with the afterlife.

Somewhere in that stew of corruption and decay, between the broken streetlights and the flickering neon, a killer roamed. They called him the Storyville Slayer, a ghost among the forgotten, a shadow preying on women society had already written off. From the late 1980s into the '90s, at least twenty-four women—mostly sex workers and addicts, the kind of people who go missing without headlines—were found strangled and dumped in swamps, canals, and abandoned lots across the city.

New Orleans, of course, barely flinched. The cops had enough on their hands dealing with the city's staggering murder rate, which at the time made the place feel less like a functioning metropolis and more like a live-action crime novel where the plot had spiraled out of control. This wasn't some neatly packaged, suburban boogeyman like the Zodiac Killer or BTK—this was a predator who operated in the margins of a city already half-drowned in its own filth.

The bodies turned up in places no sane person would go after dark—along Chef Menteur Highway, in the fetid, gator-infested waters outside the city, dumped like roadkill with barely a whisper of justice to follow. The police did what police do in cities like this: they shrugged, they stalled, they made promises no one believed.

In 1995, they had a suspect—Victor Gant, an NOPD officer with a mean streak and a suspicious connection to two of the murdered women. The kind of man whose badge gave him cover for things that would land any other street-level predator in Angola Prison for life. But charges never stuck. Maybe it was lack of evidence, or maybe it was the same grim truth as always: when it comes to murder in New Orleans, some lives don't count as much as others.

The killings continued. The city swallowed more bodies, and the Storyville Slayer dissolved into the legend of a place where death is just another item on the menu. Some say the killer was never only one man but a string of predators working the same hunting ground. Others believe he's still out there, lost in the dark corners of a city that never stopped feeding on its own.

If you make it through your visit without collapsing from exhaustion, voodoo curses, or alcohol poisoning, take a quiet walk through Lafayette Cemetery No. 1. The tombs are stacked above ground like stone apartment complexes for the dead, and the whole place feels like it's one bad storm away from waking up. It's beautiful, eerie, and a reminder that New Orleans doesn't just embrace its ghosts—it throws them a damn parade.

BATON ROUGE, LOUISIANA

Sean Vincent Gillis—aka the Other Baton Rouge Killer
Kills: 8
Span of Activity: March 1994 to February 2004

Baton Rouge is not a city for the faint of heart. It's overflowing with the faint dream of politics, petrochemicals, and bayou mysticism, wrapped in a thick cloud of humidity and the scent of deep-fried bad decisions. If you find yourself here, whether by accident or some twisted stroke of fate, there are a few key things you need to know.

First, let's talk about booze. Baton Rouge has no shortage of soulless sports bars and overpriced "cocktail lounges" where political aides and washed-up lobbyists gather like buzzards on a bloated carcass. Avoid them. You want the real Baton Rouge, the kind of place where the floor is sticky, the jukebox is angry, and the bartender looks like he just got out on parole.

At some point, the alcohol will betray you, and you'll need grease, spice, and something that won't ask too many questions. Find yourself a gas station selling boudin. It's a Cajun sausage packed with rice, pork, and a hint of danger—pure Louisiana survival food. Eat it standing up, preferably while staring into the abyss of the Mississippi River, contemplating your life choices.

Enter Sean Vincent Gillis.

Born in 1962, Gillis was not the kind of lunatic who made a spectacle of himself. No grandiose rants, no Manson-like charisma, no desperate need to be feared. He was the worst kind of predator—the invisible kind. A quiet, greasy nobody who blended into the background, a man you wouldn't notice unless he wanted you to.

Unlike his fellow Baton Rouge killer, Derrick Todd Lee, a smooth-talking charmer who preyed on women like a bayou Casanova, Gillis was a different breed of psychopath. He was a self-professed computer nerd, an overgrown mama's boy who lived at home until his thirties, a man who spent his nights watching pornography and lurking in the shadows, waiting for the right moment to strike.

Between 1994 and 2003, Gillis prowled the streets of Baton Rouge like a starving wolf, hunting women who had the misfortune of crossing his path. He wasn't picky—sex workers, joggers, single mothers—anyone who was vulnerable enough to overpower. His victims weren't just killed; they were mutilated, defiled, and discarded like roadside garbage.

By the time the Baton Rouge PD put the puzzle pieces together, Gillis had been butchering women for nearly a decade. He was caught in 2004 after DNA evidence linked him to the killings. No high-speed chases, no blaze of glory—just a dull-eyed man sitting in an interrogation room, confessing to horrors that would make even the most hardened cop queasy. Gillis is spending the rest of his days incarcerated at the Louisiana State Penitentiary.

When you're done visiting Mr. Gillis' stomping ground—or rather, hunting ground—and you've sweated through your clothes and need a bizarre break from reality, head to The Myrtles Plantation, about thirty-three miles north in St. Francisville. They say it's one of the most haunted places in America, but that's just tourism bait. The real horror aren't the ghosts; it's the existential dread of realizing that antebellum Louisiana still clings to life like an alligator on a chicken bone. Stay the night if you dare, but don't expect to sleep—between the creaky wooden floors, the distant wails of the swamp, and the relentless spirits of the past, you'll be lucky to escape with your sanity intact.

JACKSONVILLE, FLORIDA

Ottis Toole
Kills: 6 convicted, 1 suspected, hundreds more claimed
Span of Activity:1961 to 1983

Jacksonville is not a city for the delicate. It's loud, sprawling, and unapologetically weird. The highways make no sense, the humidity will break you, and somewhere, right now, a man in jorts is yelling at a bartender over the results of a college football game from 1998.

But if you can handle the madness, if you can embrace the chaos, you just might find something beautiful in this sweaty, sunburned corner of America. Just don't stay too long—this place has a way of pulling you in, and before you know it, you'll be calling it home.

Jacksonville is a sprawling, sunburned reality of bad decisions, worse tattoos, and an endless parade of strip malls that look like they were built by a drunken real estate developer on a losing streak. It's the kind of place where the humidity sticks to your skin like an unpaid debt and where the locals will either welcome you with an ice-cold beer or chase you off with a rusted-out shotgun, depending on the time of day.

If you find yourself here—whether by accident, parole violation, or sheer masochistic curiosity—you'll need to know how to survive. Forget about the beaches and the sterile tourist traps; you're here for the weird, the wild, and the places where the drinks are cheap and the jukebox plays nothing but bad decisions.

And then there's Ottis Toole, God's living proof that IQs can go into negative territory.

Born in Jacksonville, Florida, in 1947, Ottis Toole was the sort of person you'd expect to be raised in a place where summer lasts nine months and everyone has a story about a cousin who was bitten by a snake. His childhood was, to put it gently, an absolute mess. His mother dressed him in girls' clothing as punishment, his grandmother was a self-proclaimed Satanist who dabbled in grave-robbing, and by the time most kids were learning how to tie their shoes, Ottis had already discovered his two greatest passions: setting fires and running away from home.

He drifted through life like a particularly unpleasant oil spill, leaving behind a trail of theft, violence, and half-eaten sandwiches. He met his soulmate, Henry Lee Lucas, in the mid-1970s, and together, they formed the sort of unholy duo that makes people lock their doors in broad daylight. Lucas, a man with one eye and an unshakable enthusiasm for lying, claimed they killed hundreds of people together. The truth is murkier. Authorities believe Toole was responsible for a number of murders, and his most infamous crime is the 1981 kidnapping and murder of Adam Walsh, the six-year-old son of *America's Most Wanted* host John Walsh.

Except, of course, he later recanted. Confessed again. Then recanted. It was as if he were testing different versions of his life, trying to decide which one fit best. Meanwhile, the police weren't much help, managing to lose his car, his murder confessions, and possibly even some of his brain cells along the way. It wasn't until 2008—long after Toole had died in prison from cirrhosis—that authorities officially closed the Adam Walsh case, deciding that yes, he probably did it.

Before you leave Jacksonville, if you want to see something truly strange, something that will stick with you like a bad acid trip, you need to make your way to Skunk Ape Headquarters.

Yes, you heard that right. Florida's own Bigfoot—the Skunk Ape—has a shrine of sorts just south of Jacksonville, where believers and lunatics alike gather to swap stories, examine blurry photos, and buy t-shirts that say, "I Believe." The place is run by a man who claims to have seen the creature himself, and he will happily sell you books, bumper stickers, and a healthy dose of paranoia. Even if you don't believe in the Skunk Ape, you should at least pay your respects—it's not every day you find a roadside attraction dedicated to a mythical beast that smells like a wet possum on a hot day.

GAINESVILLE, FLORIDA

Danny Rolling—aka the Gainesville Ripper
Kills: 8
Span of Activity: 1989 to August 1990

Gainesville, Florida—a town where the air smells like spilled beer and fried food, where the locals have mastered the fine art of day drinking, and where college football is a full-blown religious experience. This is the heart of Gator Country, a strange and lawless place where the line between genius and complete insanity is as thin as the sweat-stained tank tops worn by the town's perpetual undergrad population.

Avoid the obvious, stay away from the frat houses unless you enjoy the sound of someone vomiting at noon, and for the love of all that is holy, don't engage in an argument about Florida football unless you have three hours to kill and a death wish.

Every college town has a few bars that refuse to die, places where the alcohol is cheap, the bathrooms are a crime scene, and the regulars look like they haven't seen sunlight since the Clinton administration. In Gainesville, that bar is The Blarney Stone.

This is not the place for a fancy cocktail or a quiet conversation. No, The Blarney Stone is where you go to drink whiskey out of plastic cups while some guy in a Lynyrd Skynyrd shirt tells you about the time he almost made it as a roadie. The floors are beer-stained, the jukebox is hostile, and if you make eye contact with the wrong person, you may end up in a debate about whether Tim Tebow was actually a prophet. But if you can handle it, if you can withstand the madness, you'll find that this is the real Gainesville—loud, unpolished, and utterly unapologetic.

Onto the Gainesville Ripper.

Danny Rolling, a man whose life choices read like the plot of a horror movie written by someone who had just sustained a head injury.

Born in 1954 in Shreveport, Louisiana, Rolling was the kind of child who made neighbors lock their doors during the daytime. His father, a police officer with the emotional depth of a cinder block, spent much of Rolling's childhood reminding him that he was unwanted, often using fists, insults, and the occasional boot to drive the point home. This did not foster an atmosphere of warmth or stability. Instead, Rolling spent his teenage years floundering between petty crime, religious guilt, and a deepening fascination with violent fantasies—a trifecta that, historically speaking, never ends well.

By the late 1980s, Rolling had amassed a colorful résumé of armed robberies, prison stints, and a failed attempt at playing house with a wife who left him after he held a gun to her head. Heartbroken and increasingly detached from reality, he did what so many men do after a breakup: he started murdering people.

In August 1990, Rolling set his sights on Gainesville, Florida, a town where cheap beer flows freely and the University of Florida's student population is too busy worrying about midterms and football to notice a man skulking around with a hunting knife. Over the course of four days, he brutally murdered five students, posing their bodies in grotesque positions as if arranging furniture in a crime scene-themed IKEA catalog.

The details of his crimes were straight out of a slasher film—forced entry, mutilation, decapitation, and an artistic flourish that suggested Rolling was less interested in murder and more interested in directing a one-man horror production where he played every role. Gainesville, understandably, lost its collective mind. Students fled campus, parents arrived in rental cars to scoop up their traumatized children, and the town's local hardware stores made a fortune selling deadbolts and pepper spray.

Rolling, meanwhile, was completely unaware of the chaos he had caused. By the time police connected him to the killings, he was already sitting in jail for robbing a Winn-Dixie, which, if nothing else, is an aggressively Florida way to get caught.

If you want to see something truly bizarre, something that will stick with you long after the hangover fades, head over to Devil's Millhopper Geological State Park. It's a massive, gaping sinkhole that looks like Mother Nature decided to give up and swallow an entire chunk of the town.

Legend has it that the sinkhole was formed when the Devil himself lured a bunch of women to their doom, but the reality is somehow even stranger. Walk down the rickety wooden stairs and you'll find yourself in a prehistoric jungle, complete with waterfalls, strange sounds, and the unsettling feeling that you've stepped into a place where time works differently. It's humid, eerie, and exactly the kind of place where you'd expect to stumble upon a lost Florida Man still trying to find his way home.

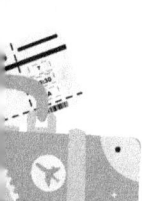

MIAMI, FLORIDA

Miami Strangler
Kills: 9–11
Span of Activity: August 1964 to
October 1970

The only thing more South than Miami is the Florida Keys, and to be honest, no one in their right mind would associate the Keys with Florida.

Welcome to Miami. The city where cocaine dreams meet sunburnt reality, where the humidity wraps around you like a wet python, and the neon lights flicker like some kind of electric voodoo spell. If you've come looking for peace, turn back now. This place is a high-speed blender of Latin heat, gator-infested swamps, and people so beautiful they'll make you reconsider every life choice you've ever made.

No trip to Miami is complete without a pilgrimage to Coral Castle, a bizarre limestone structure built by a lovesick Latvian madman named Edward Leedskalnin. He carved and assembled the entire thing—1,100 tons of coral rock—alone, in secret, using methods nobody fully understands. Some say he knew the secrets of the pyramids; others say he had supernatural strength or struck a deal with the Devil. Either way, he spent decades on this strange, lonesome love letter to a woman who never showed up. If that's not Miami energy, I don't know what is.

Miami in the late '80s was a seething hotbed of cocaine wars, neon excess, and bodies washing up in the bay. Amidst the chaos, whispers began circulating about a shadowy figure stalking the underbelly of the city—a predator who preyed on the vulnerable and left behind only cold bodies and a lingering

air of dread. The media, always hungry for fear, dubbed him the Miami Strangler.

His victims—drifters, nightclub workers, and the kind of people who disappear without headlines—were all found with telltale ligature marks around their throats. Some were posed in strange, almost ritualistic ways. There were no signs of struggle, no witnesses, just a ghost moving through the night. The killer's calling card? A silk tie, often expensive, sometimes monogrammed, left behind like a signature on a contract.

Despite a wave of paranoia and a full-scale manhunt, the Strangler was never caught. Some believe he was a former hitman for the cartels who took pleasure in a more personal style of murder. Others claim he was a disillusioned businessman, snapping under the weight of Miami's relentless excess. A few even whisper that he never left—that he simply evolved, got smarter, and still walks among us.

Now that you've walked the streets of Miami, knowing that the Miami Strangler is possibly still out there, you could use a drink. You want authenticity? You want a place where the beer is cold, the cash is king, and the walls reek of cigar smoke and lost nights? Mac's Club Deuce is the promised land. This dive bar has been standing since 1926, long before South Beach became an Instagram circus. Inside, it's dark, dirty, and drenched in sin. The neon glow makes everyone look just a little more dangerous, and the drinks are strong enough to make you believe you can outswim an alligator. Anthony Bourdain drank here. Strippers, bikers, washed-up gangsters, and lost tourists stumble in at odd hours. You should too.

GREAT LAKES REGION

As you continue your macabre journey across this great nation, make sure to give yourself plenty of time to explore the Great Lakes region, one of the most beautiful areas in the country. If summertime adventures are your jam, the Great Lakes region of the United States may very well be the best area in the entire nation to check out. Whether camping in a tent or an RV, you will find plenty of places to rest your head for the night. Depending on where you choose and how deeply you sleep, you'll have a fairly good chance of waking up in the morning. Thousands of ships have sunk over the years in the Great Lakes, with many still missing and considered ghost ships. What goes on underneath the surface of the waters of these vast lakes is largely unknown, just as unknown as what lies beneath the surface of many of these vicious killers.

Our trip starts in Ohio, home to burning rivers, collapsing cities, and corrupt politicians. We move on to Michigan, where every resident has either hit a deer, worked for General Motors, or has been in prison. Next, we travel to Indiana, known as a great place to live if you don't care about public education or women's rights, and these days, who does?

Then we head to Illinois, known for the great city of Chicago and, well, that's pretty much it, unless we're talking about brutal winters, high taxes, and corruption. Finally, we wind our way through Wisconsin, which is the only place in the world where liking cheese curds, the Packers, and Miller Lite will get you laid.

If you're not a tourist and have lived in the Great Lakes region for a while, you may have witnessed some of the most atrocious acts in American history. Some of our nation's most brutal killers—such as Samuel Little, Jeffrey Dahmer, and John Wayne Gacy—all hail from this area.

Enjoy yourself as you take in the glory of this region, but remember that even in the most beautiful places, darkness still lives.

CLEVELAND, OHIO

Anthony Sowell—aka the
Cleveland Strangler
Kills: 11
Span of Activity: May 2007 to
September 2009

Fun Fact: During his seven-year Marine Corps career, Sowell received a Good Conduct medal

Let's begin our trip in Cleveland, Ohio. Once considered by many a place to avoid, Cleveland is now on its way back up with a vengeance. Just kidding. It's awful there. Unless of course you consider conversations about the Cleveland Browns, cornhole, or corned beef interesting.

On your visit to this great city, you might begin the day at the Cleveland Museum of Art, or perhaps you'll take a trip to the West Side Public Market. Then at night, you could check out the city's thriving food-and-drink scene before attending a play in the theatre district. If theatre isn't your jam, perhaps head to Lake Erie for lively music and lovely views.

Just make sure you're back at your hotel at night. Cleveland isn't known as the Mistake by the Lake for nothing.

Part of the city's dark history is a man named Anthony Sowell, also known as the Cleveland Strangler. He was born in Cleveland to a single mother who abused Sowell severely. She was known to strip her young son naked, tie him up, and brutally beat him. When he graduated from high school, he joined the military, where he served as a United States Marine for seven years. When he was discharged, he moved back to Cleveland. Because why not?

Hmm, let's see: poverty, an abusive parent, and a stint in the military. I wonder what's going to happen next?

In 1989, the mask began to slip off. Sowell tied up and attempted to rape a woman who visited him in his home. In 1990 he was charged with kidnapping, rape, and attempted rape. He pled guilty to attempted rape, and served fifteen years in prison. In 2005, he was released from prison, moved back to Cleveland, because why the fuck not, and found a job in a factory.

Sowell lived in a house on the corner of Imperial Avenue and East 123rd Street. Many people in the neighborhood began to notice the area around his house smelled bad; in fact, the home had an odor so awful that they began to complain. Lucky for Sowell, but not for his future victims, the blame for this overpowering stink was cast on a business next door called Ray's Sausage. City officials forced the company to pay thirty thousand dollars to fix their sewage and ventilation systems. This situation contributed to the age-old question: decomposing bodies or sausage?

Yet the smell remained. And women continued to disappear.

Rumors began circulating about the man who lived in the house that smelled like death. One day, a woman named Latundra Billups went to his house to smoke some crack. This wasn't a good idea for a variety of reasons, but in theory, using crack is a pretty good time, and I'm not here to judge.

While there, she got so incredibly high, she asked if there was any proof to the rumors that Sowell was the guy who'd been attacking all sorts of neighborhood women. As soon as the words were out of her mouth, Sowell hit her, which pretty much answered her question. He then raped her and used an extension cord to strangle her unconscious.

When she woke up, she said Sowell looked surprised.

Wouldn't you be?

She managed to escape and reported Sowell to the police. A few days later, police came to the house to investigate. Sowell had been busy. They found two bodies buried in the basement and four others in crawl spaces on the third floor. More bodies were found when investigators dug up the backyard. All were local women who struggled with poverty and drug use.

Sowell was charged with eleven counts of murder as well as rape, attempted murder, tampering with evidence, and abuse of a corpse. He was convicted and sentenced to death. He died in 2021 from a terminal illness while still incarcerated. It couldn't have happened to a nicer guy.

While in the city, check out the Buckland Museum of Witchcraft and Magic; it is billed as "Cleveland's most unique tourist destination."

I'm going to take it a step further: it's pretty unique there are tourists in Cleveland at all.

ASHLAND, OHIO

Shawn Grate
Kills: 5+
Span of Activity: 2006 to 2016

As you leave Cleveland, it's just a bit over an hour down I-71 to our next stop, Ashland, Ohio, the home of Shawn Grate. And not much else.

The only thing possibly worse than living in Cleveland is living in a suburb of Cleveland. You know you're in Ashland if it's okay to tell racist jokes because you have a Black friend and you get invited to around five cookouts a month. Ashland is known as the "balloon capital of the world," which is obviously a huge lie. Still, each summer, many come to see the BalloonFest.

Shawn Grate was said to be very charming growing up. One of his former high school friends once said that "all the girls liked Shawn."

Well, maybe they did for a little while. When still in high school, he was arrested for grabbing his girlfriend's throat, which possibly made her, and others, not like Shawn that much after all. Once out of high school, Grate was caught breaking into a house to steal jewelry and money. He was sentenced to four years in prison for burglary.

Once released, it seemed Grate was keeping his nose clean and had learned his lesson. But in reality, he was slaughtering women left and right.

This all came to an end after a woman Grate had kidnapped, bound to a bed, and held hostage for three days managed to call 911 while Grate slept. While held captive, the woman was repeatedly brutally sexually assaulted. Grate even shaved a heart shape into her pubic hair. Grate, a true romantic, claims he did not plan to kill her and that they were going to get married.

Somehow, I doubt that.

When officers searched Grate's home, they found the bodies of two women. Grate later admitted to three more murders. He strangled all his victims.

While in jail awaiting trial, Grate sent a letter to a Cleveland news station in which he wrote that government assistance was the reason for all of this. Of his victims, he wrote, "They were already dead, just their bodies were flopping wherever it can flop but their minds were already dead! The state took their minds. Once they started receiving their monthly checks." It's unclear if he also thought these women were taking Americans' jobs and eating dogs.

Grate has been sentenced to death. It is scheduled for some time in 2025.

On your way out of town, check out the Ashland Antique Tractor and Engine Show. Held the second weekend in July, the show features a different brand of tractor each year. This isn't a tractor competition, just the best tractor show possible for the benefit of the most people. Because if you didn't know, people like tractors. Anyone who has an interest in farm and power equipment of the past will enjoy this one-of-a-kind show.

YPSILANTI, MICHIGAN

John Collins—aka the Ypsilanti Ripper
Kills: 7+
Span of Activity: July 1967 to March 1969

Fun Fact: Collins was kicked out of his fraternity at Eastern Michigan University for stealing

As we continue our trip, let's drive northwest to Ypsilanti, Michigan, home to Eastern Michigan University.

Known for its historic architecture and museums, Ypsilanti has a bohemian feel with unique shops, restaurants, and breweries. As the home of Eastern Michigan, it's also home to declining enrollment, binge drinking, and date rapes. Ypsilanti is known by "Ypsi" by the locals, because when on a meth binge, typing four more letters matters.

The Michigan Murders were a series of killings of young women and girls committed between 1967 and 1969 around the Ypsilanti area. The killer was known by a variety of names, including the Ypsilanti Ripper, the Michigan Murderer, and the Co-Ed Killer. All the victims were between the ages of thirteen and twenty-one. They were abducted, raped, and beaten before they were killed. Usually, they were strangled to death.

The first victim was Mary Fleszar, who disappeared from the campus of Eastern Michigan University. Her body was found about a month afterward. While her remains were at the mortuary, a friendly young man showed up and asked to take some pictures of her body. He claimed Mary's parents had asked him to do so. This is perfectly normal, of course. Most parents tend to have mortuary pictures of their offspring framed and hung by the fireplace. When the mortuary staff told him that wasn't going to happen, he asked, "You mean you can't fix her up enough so I could just get one picture of her?"

A year later, Joan Schell went missing; she was found five days later, raped, and stabbed an estimated forty-seven times. She was last seen with John Collins, a student at EMU. He was questioned by police but let go. Apparently, the police thought Collins was not a forty-seven-stabs kind of guy.

Eight months later, three other victims were killed in a matter of weeks. One was strangled and shot in the head, one bludgeoned to death, and another, only thirteen years old, was strangled with an electrical cord.

The next to meet her end at the hands of the Ypsilanti Ripper was Alice Kalom, found in a vacant field. She had been raped repeatedly before her throat was slashed and she was shot in the head. The final victim, Karen Beineman, went missing from her dorm at EMU a few weeks later.

One thing that kept coming up around all these murders was just how plain *weird* John Collins was. He spent a lot of time talking to his female coworkers about the crime, describing in great detail all the horrible things that were done to the victims. When asked how he knew so much about the killings, he said he was told them by his uncle, David Leik, who was a sergeant on the local police force.

Speaking of David Leik. One day, he returned to his home in Ypsilanti after a family vacation and noticed black paint spilled on his basement floor. He figured it must have been caused by his nephew John Collins, who had been taking care of the dog while Leik and his family were away on vacation.

Now, let's be clear: if you're in the midst of a long murder spree, accepting a gig watching the dog of someone in the state police is probably not the best idea. Leik was later told that Collins had been questioned in connection with the murders. He went home and scraped away the paint only to see underneath there were brown stains on the floor.

When the stains were studied at the state police lab, they turned out to be nothing but varnish. But when Leik had scraped up the paint, he moved the washing machine and found some hair. When he brought the hair to the lab, it turned out to be a match to Karen Beineman.

Collins was arrested. He was tried and convicted of the Beineman murder and is currently serving a life sentence. He maintains his innocence and has numerous female pen pals.

On the way out of town, check out the World of Rocks, your source for rare fossils, colorful minerals, and a selection of crystals that will blow your mind. Whether you're a hardcore rock aficionado (and who isn't when it comes down to it?) or you want a beautiful piece of the Earth to take with you, check out the World of Rocks, one of the largest rock shops in Michigan.

EAST LANSING, MICHIGAN

Don Miller—aka the East Lansing
Serial Killer
Kills: 5
Span of Activity: December 1977
to August 1978

Fun Fact: Miller was a youth minister in high school

An hour or so northwest of Ypsilanti is our next stop, East Lansing, Michigan. East Lansing, like many college towns, is known for its arts and culture as well as its restaurants, bars, and breweries. Well, that's what it's known for if you're a college student at Michigan State University. Residents know East Lansing as a place where the heat usually doesn't work in your studio apartment. East Lansing has both a small-town feel and a bustling downtown. By "small town," I mean there isn't anything to do, and "bustling" is a synonym for "run, that guy's got a knife!"

In late 1976, Don Miller proposed to Martha Sue Young, whom he'd been going out with since high school.

She said yes!

Sadly for Miller and Young, as it turned out, she broke up with him before they were married. This made him real mad. Miller convinced her to meet with him for a talk on New Year's Eve 1977. It was time to let the love of his life know his true feelings.

It obviously didn't go the way he hoped. He strangled her to death that night, and the East Lansing Serial Killer was born.

When Young didn't return home, her parents contacted the police. Miller admitted that he had been with her most of the night, but drove her home at around two a.m., dropped her off, and left. On October 20, 1977, two hunters found Young's clothes and purse near a lake in Bath, Michigan.

In June 1978, Miller murdered twenty-seven-year-old Marita Choquette, whom he stabbed seventeen times. After killing her, he posed her body and cut off her hands, although maybe it was in the opposite order. Over the next few weeks, he killed two more victims.

He wasn't done.

In August, Miller knocked on the door of a house in Lansing, ostensibly to use the phone. The door was opened by fourteen-year-old Lisa Gilbert, who was alone in the house. These were the old days, when a fourteen-year-old would immediately open her door to any odd-looking psychotic who happened on by. Miller beat her, tied her up, and was in the process of raping her when he was confronted by her thirteen-year-old brother who'd just come home. This allowed Lisa to run outside, naked except for some nylon stockings and one of her dad's neckties, which was being used as a gag. Miller drove off, like the big coward he was, but numerous witnesses saw his license plate.

He was arrested at his apartment and charged with rape and attempted murder. He was found guilty and sentenced to fifty years in prison. He later pleaded guilty to the other four murders. His projected release date is March 24, 2031, a few short years away.

If you're kicking around East Lansing, check out Pinball Pete's, where they have a ton of pinball machines, old-school video games, and new-school state-of-the-art games as well. If you think you've got what it takes, you can even join the East Lansing Pinball League. They're open until two a.m. on Fridays and Saturdays.

WESTFIELD, INDIANA

Herb Baumeister—aka the I-70 Strangler
Kills: 24+
Span of Activity: June1980 to 1995

If one were to head a few hundred miles to the southwest from East Lansing, one might come across the town of Westfield, Indiana. Westfield was founded in 1834 by North Carolina Quakers. It is believed that the town was initially planned as a stop on the Underground Railroad, which makes sense as escaping from slavery is pretty much the only reason someone would stop here.

There's no shortage of activities in family-friendly Westfield. Actually, there's an enormous shortage, but I have word count to think of. Take a historic ghost walk tour or hit the greens at the revered Wood Wind Golf Club. If you've got time, spend a leisurely afternoon in Cool Creek Park, perfect for hiking, jogging, and birdwatching.

You want to go birdwatching, right?

You could also visit the former home of Herb Baumeister, also known as the I-70 Strangler.

Baumeister's childhood was apparently normal, but in his early teen years, he started seeming a bit odd, doing things like playing with dead animals and urinating on a teacher's desk. To be clear, urinating on a teacher's desk is no big thing, but combined with the dead animals, it's odd AF. As a teenager, he was diagnosed with schizophrenia and antisocial personality disorder but did not receive further psychiatric treatment. Why bother?

He married in 1971, a union that produced three children. His wife later said they had sex only six times in over twenty-five years. But who is counting? She never saw Herb naked for their entire marriage, which unfortunately makes me wonder what happened the six times they banged. Was he wearing a T-shirt? A three-piece suit?

A lot of gay men began disappearing around this time, and detectives began to think the crimes were related. In 1993, they spoke to a witness who claimed a man named Brian Smart had killed a friend of his and had tried to kill him as well. The witness had seen "Brian Smart" around town and gave the police the suspect's license plate. The police soon found that Brian Smart was, in fact, Herb Baumeister.

They went to Baumeister's home, told him he was a suspect in the disappearances, and asked to search his house. Baumeister refused, as did his wife.

A year or so later, Baumeister's wife had seemingly had enough of this dangerous oddball and filed for divorce. She also told the police to go ahead and search the house while her erstwhile husband was away for a few days.

The cops found the remains of eleven men buried around the property.

Baumeister took off to Ontario, where he died by suicide at Pinery Provincial Park. In his suicide note, he wrote that he regretted his suicide might mess up the park. Caring about others until the end.

In addition to the murders at his estate, Baumeister is also strongly suspected of killing nine more men, who were found near Interstate 70 in Indiana and Ohio between Indianapolis and Columbus.

While you're in Westfield, check out the Four Finger Distillery, where you can get some of the best bourbon, vodka, or absinthe one can find anywhere. The distillery got its name from the time its distiller and owner, Brad, cut off one of his fingers with a saw. If you'd like a distillery tour, they do that. Just give them forty-eight hours' notice, please and thank you.

HAMMOND, INDIANA

Rudy Bladel—aka the Railway Killer
Kills: 7
Span of Activity: August 1963 to December 1978

Fun Fact: Bladel claimed he had an IQ of 145

A few hours northwest of Westfield is Hammond, Indiana. Hammond boasts some terrific attractions and entertainment options, including casino gambling and exhibits at the state-of-the-art Indiana Welcome Center. Nothing says good gambling like a welcome center.

If you're into trains, Hammond is also a cool place to check out the tracks of the Indiana Harbor Belt Railroad. Hammond is also a cool place if you're into population decline, a lack of amenities, and crippling depression.

Rudy Bladel, aka the Railway Sniper, loved the railroad. His father was a fireman for the railroad in Chicago, Illinois, and Bladel's dream as a child was to follow in his footsteps. He was hired at the same railroad company his father worked for and was as happy as could be. Well, he was happy until he was laid off after the railroad decided to move to Elkhart, Indiana.

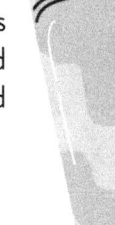

Then he went out of his mind.

On August 3, 1963, Bladel shot engineer Roy Bottorf and his fireman, Paul Overstreet, to death in the cab of their train. The crime remained unsolved. It was nearly forgotten when the killer struck a second time, five years later, when engineer John Marshall was shot to death on his train in Elkhart. The police had no suspects. Why would they? What kind of oddball has train envy anyway?

Three years later, Bladel shot yet another engineer in the same railroad yard. This time, his purported victim fought back and disarmed Bladel, who was soon arrested. He pleaded guilty to aggravated battery and was sentenced to one to five years in prison. He served eighteen months and was paroled in 1973. He was suspected of the other crimes, but there was nothing to pin them on him.

If you thought that was the end of the story, you were wrong. Bladel was on a mission. A mission that apparently didn't involve any self-awareness or sense of shame.

On April 5, 1976, James McCrory was seated in his locomotive in the yard at Elkhart when he was shot dead through its window.

This time, Bladel was suspected immediately.

He needed to find a new location to kill. Well, actually, what he needed to do was get his shit together but that wasn't going to happen.

On New Year's Eve 1978, he carried a shotgun into the railyards in Jackson, Michigan, where he shot flagman Robert Blake, and William Gulak, a conductor. He then shot and killed Charles Burton, a railroad fireman, as he arrived for work.

While Bladel was held for questioning about the Jackson massacre, he was released for lack of solid evidence. Who knows, maybe there was some other dude walking around killing railroad workers for no reason.

Three months later, some hikers found Bladel's shotgun in a park outside of Jackson. The gun was traced to back to him. He was booked for triple murder on March 22, 1979, and confessed to the Jackson crimes. Bladel drew three consecutive life terms in prison. He died of cancer in 2006, all the while wondering why no one choo-choo-chose him to work at the railroad of his choice.

Before you get out of town, maybe choo-choo-choose to spend some time at Horseshoe Hammond. Sure, it's crowded as Hell, and you have to wait in line for the bathroom for twenty minutes, but don't worry, you can chain smoke the entire time.

CHICAGO, ILLINOIS

Andrew Cunnanan
Kills: 5
Span of Activity: April 27 to July 15, 1997

Fun Fact: He was voted "most likely to not be forgotten" in high school

If you leave Hammond and drive north for thirty miles or so, you'll reach Chicago, the next stop on our tour. Chicago is undeniably one of the coolest cities in the world. While many come for Chicago-style hot dogs, deep-dish pizza, and Polish sausage, others come for the long commutes, high crime rates, poor public schools, and real estate foreclosures.

Dude, that Polish sausage is dope though.

Chicago has many museums, including the Art Institute of Chicago, and is home to the world's first skyscraper, which was built in 1885. Just don't look up at it too long, lest someone hits you upside the head with a brick.

At the time of his crimes, Andrew Cunanan was a twenty-seven-year-old college dropout from California. He was highly intelligent, spoke two languages, and was charming as all get out.

Since his teenage years, Cunanan sought a life of luxury, but he certainly didn't want to work for it. He was a rent boy of sorts, acting as a "live-in boyfriend" to a series of older men who would make sure he lived the lifestyle he desired by taking him on vacations and buying him gifts. Nice work if you can get it, right? Sure, banging someone you despise isn't pleasant but look at that fucking view!

For reasons that remain unclear, Cunanan went totally off his head in late April 1997.

First, he killed a "friend" of his with a hammer in Minneapolis. A few days later, he shot and killed an architect in Minnesota.

On May 3, Cunanan drove to Chicago and killed seventy-two-year-old real estate investor Lee Miglin. He bound his hands and feet, wrapped his head with duct tape, then stabbed him more than twenty times, slit his throat, and stole his car. Those who knew Miglin claim the killing was random, but many in law enforcement feel differently. Less than a week later, Cunanan killed a cemetery worker in New Jersey and took his truck.

Authorities soon figured out that Cunanan was the culprit for these crimes. The story hit the national news. Everyone was looking for him.

But he seemed to have vanished.

On the morning of July 15, 1997, Gianni Versace, one of the most famous fashion designers in the world, returned home to his Miami Beach mansion after taking a walk. Cunnanan, weird as Hell to the end, walked up behind Versace and shot him twice in the back of the head, killing him instantly.

A few days later, the caretaker of a houseboat reported hearing a gunshot. Responders found Cunanan on the boat, dead from a self-inflicted wound. His killing spree was over.

The good times aren't over at Wrigley Field, however. While in Chicago, check out a behind-the-scenes look at the legendary home of the Chicago Cubs with Wrigley Field Tours. Built in 1914, this must-see Chicago attraction houses more than one hundred years of history, most of which have been undeniably awful.

STREAMWOOD, ILLINOIS

Paul Runge
Kills: 8+
Span of Activity: January 1995 to
March 1997

Fun Fact: Runge once worked as a shoe salesman

Twenty miles from Aurora sits Streamwood, a suburb of Chicago. The village is best known for having ample attractions and things to do. Although no one is quite sure what those things to do *actually* are. Streamwood grew roots in the post-World War II suburban expansion, which transformed it from rural farmland to a vibrant, residential community. Who needs nature when you can have a Chipotle!

Not much is known about Runge's childhood. When he was seventeen, he kidnapped and raped a fourteen-year-old girl. After he was paroled in May 1994, he married a woman named Charlene. She soon played a role in some of Runge's evil proclivities, but whether she was a willing participant or another victim is still unknown.

Runge's first victim, Stacy Frobel, was an acquaintance of Runge's wife. She went to visit Charlene in the couple's home and was never seen alive afterwards. Runge killed her by hitting her with a dumbbell; then he cut up her body in the bathtub, using a saw. A few weeks after her visit, a German shepherd, who was obviously not a good boy, brought a severed leg home to its owner. A few weeks later, it brought the other leg back. DNA tests concluded that it was Stacy Frobel.

Next to be slaughtered by this psychopath were Dženeta and Amela Pašanbegovi. The two were sisters, last seen on July 11, 1995, when they were offered a house cleaning job by the Runges. They must have missed a few dust bunnies, because

THE SERIAL KILLER TRAVEL GUIDE ACROSS AMERICA   173

once in the home, they were raped and strangled to death.

Killing people in his house probably didn't seem to be a good long-term plan so Runge branched out. In January 1997, he raped and strangled to death thirty-year-old Dorota Dziubak in her home. Runge had ostensibly come by in response to an ad for her selling her house.

In February, he responded to another "for sale" ad and murdered a forty-year-old woman, Yolanda Gutierrez, and her ten-year-old daughter, Jessica Muniz. After slitting their throats, he burned their house to the ground.

A month later, Kazimiera Paruch, forty-three, similarly encountered Runge when he expressed interest in buying her condo. He raped and strangled her. Firefighters found her body after extinguishing the fire in her home. Law enforcement was suspicious of Runge and his creepy wife. After all, multiple women had disappeared who were last seen at their home. On March 8, 1996, the FBI searched the Runge house. While they didn't find anything incriminating when it came to the murders, they found a crossbow, a stun gun, and a knife, which was enough to bust him on possession of a weapon, a violation of his parole.

Soon afterwards, DNA evidence linked Runge to the "want ad" murders. He subsequently confessed to five murders, but he is a suspect in many others. Charlene Runge was granted immunity in exchange for her cooperation.

In January 2006, Runge was convicted of the Gutierrez-Muniz murders and was sentenced to death. His sentence was later commuted to life in prison.

While in Streamwood, check out Dotty's! They offer a fun, friendly atmosphere for gaming and slots in a conveniently located shopping center. As we all know, playing slots in a small room adjacent to a strip mall is the best. While there, check out their food menu full of comfort classics!

AURORA, ILLINOIS

Bruce Lindahl
Kills: 12+
Span of Activity: 1976 to April 1981

Aurora has many attractions, including museums, theaters, outdoor activities, and shopping. This somewhat detracts from its bad schools, high crime rates, and empty storefronts. During the heat of summer, check out Splash Country Water Park, the largest water park in the entire state of Illinois. The rest of the year, residents replicate the water park experience with all the flooding in the area.

Bruce Lindahl was born on January 29, 1953, in St. Charles, Illinois. He graduated college with a degree in electromechanics and worked as an electrician as a young man. His friends said he was chill, for the most part, but occasionally he showed signs of aggression and impulsivity.

You think?

Lindahl had some issues. In his early twenties, he began to commit numerous minor criminal offenses and was repeatedly arrested, but he never got any jail time. In 1979, he invited twenty-year-old Annette Lazar to his house, pretending he had some weed to sell her. Instead, he raped her at gunpoint, which probably would have been even worse if she was stoned. Talk about harshing someone's mellow. Lindahl was not charged with any crime.

Shortly afterwards, Lindahl was pulled over by the police for a traffic infraction. The police discovered an unconscious woman bleeding from her head in the back seat of the car. Lindahl claimed that he was taking her to the hospital, but if he was, he was going the wrong way. An examination showed the woman had been sexually assaulted. Lindahl had given her a drink at a party and she blacked out. Again, no charges were filed.

He kept at it. Why wouldn't he? The dude is literally raping chicks left and right and nothing happened to him.

Might as well up the ante a bit.

On January 12, 1976, the body of sixteen-year-old Pamela Maurer was found on a road behind a guardrail. She had been raped and strangled. Three years later, the body of nineteen-year-old Kathy Halle was discovered in the Fox River near North Aurora after she had been missing for almost a month.

On June 23, 1980, Lindahl abducted twenty-five-year-old Debra Colliander from the parking lot of a shopping center in Aurora, Illinois. He took her to his apartment, where he raped her. After Lindahl fell asleep, Colliander was able to escape. This time, the cops arrested him. Lindahl was released on bail. Shortly afterwards, Colliander went missing, and the charges were dropped as the case depended on her testimony. Her body was later found in a cornfield.

On April 4, 1981, Lindahl was hanging out with eighteen-year-old Charles Robert "Chuck" Huber when Lindahl attacked Huber with a knife, fatally stabbing him a total of twenty-eight times. No one is sure why Huber was attacked, but either way, during the murder, Lindahl accidentally severed his own femoral artery, causing his death.

It's cool the guy died but come on. Apparently, the only one who could stop Lindahl was Lindahl. The cops sure weren't going to.

News reports about Lindahl caused many women to call the police saying he had attacked or raped them previously. DNA has been used over the past few years to link Lindahl to the murder of Maurer and Halle.

On the way out of town, check out the Aurora Skate Center. If you ask nicely, they might play "Get Down on It."

NORWOOD PARK, ILLINOIS

John Wayne Gacy—aka the Killer Clown
Kills: 33+
Span of Activity: January 1972 to December 1978

Fun Fact: Gacy performed as a clown at charitable events and children's parties

Next, it's off to Norwood Park. The neighborhood was initially designed to be a resort destination with curving roads and angular streets, but stunningly, no one really GAF about vacationing in Norwood. The area used to be elite, but now it's just expensive. It's the type of area where residents spend much of their time looking out their windows, wondering if the person parked on their street is about to murder them and stick things up their ass. Not necessarily in that order.

Which brings us to John Wayne Gacy. He was born on March 17, 1942, in Chicago, Illinois. His father was an alcoholic who physically and verbally abused his son.

Gacy married into a wealthy family and relocated with his lucky bride to Waterloo, Iowa. Gacy took over management of the family's Kentucky Fried Chicken restaurant and was well-known in the community as a good, family man. I mean, not as well-known as he was in his community later, but you get the vibe. At the time, he was a member of the local Jaycees, where he would provide fried chicken and insist on being called "Colonel." That's right. You heard me.

However, all was not well with Gacy. He was arrested in 1968 for attempting to coerce a male employee into homosexual acts. At one point, telling him, "You have to have sex with a man before you start having sex with women." The validity of this point remains in question, but I'm going on record saying I don't believe that's true.

It's totally bizarre that back in the day, if you were a dude, you could get time for saying, "If you were a vegetable, you'd be a cute-cumber" to a male coworker. But this was a felony back in those days, which is incredibly messed up. But not as messed up as Gacy, who pleaded guilty to sodomy and was sentenced to ten years. His wife filed for divorce following the sentencing. She may have done this for all the wrong reasons, but I still say good on her regardless.

After serving eighteen months in prison, Gacy was paroled in 1971 and moved back to Chicago. That July, he remarried. But things didn't work out all that well, as Gacy was charged with the attempted rape of a young man. The charges were dropped when the victim failed to appear in court. The marriage didn't last. Gacy's second wife divorced him due to her husband's moodiness and obsession with homosexual magazines. *Obsession* is such a strong word, but in this case, it probably fits.

Gacy kept busy while single, spending much of his time dressing as a clown and entertaining children at local hospitals. Basically, having a grand time.

In 1978, a teenage stock boy at a local pharmacy went missing. Gacy was the last person seen with the boy before his disappearance. When investigators ran a background check on Gacy, they discovered he had previously served time for his penchant for rusty trombones. You know what they say—when there's smoke, there's fire, especially when it comes to sodomy. Investigators obtained a warrant to search Gacy's house. While searching his home, investigators entered the crawl space. A rancid odor was quickly noticed, but the smell was thought to be a sewage line. This is the kind of thing that has stumped investigators for decades: is the smell coming from a sewage line or numerous rotting corpses?

The dopey investigators found a ring during the search that belonged to a teenager who had disappeared a year earlier. Investigators were able to obtain a second search warrant for Gacy's home because of this evidence.

On December 22, 1978, Gacy, realizing that the police were going to find out what he'd been up to, confessed to thirty-three murders. Twenty-eight of those victims were buried in shallow graves under his house.

He later explained to police, "There are four Johns." John the contractor, John the clown, and John the politician. The fourth John went by the name of Jack Hanley, who was the actual killer. The police decided to settle on arresting the one John they had sitting in front of them at the time.

On March 13, 1980, Gacy was sentenced to die. Finally, fourteen years later, he was executed. His last words were "Kiss my ass." Regrettably, he didn't insist on being called Colonel.

Before you leave Norwood Park, spend some time at the Norwood Royal Cigars, which boasts the largest humidor in the Midwest. Nestled in the kind of mini mall that screams suburban opulence, their motto is "Light it! Smoke it! Love it!" And we certainly will.

MILWAUKEE, WISCONSIN

Jeffrey Dahmer—aka the
Milwaukee Monster
Kills: 17
Span of Activity: June 1978 to July
1991

Leaving Chicago, our trip takes us up 1-94 for our next stop in Milwaukee. When one thinks of Milwaukee, breweries, cultural festivals, and fabulous architecture come to mind. Well, that's what comes to mind if you work for the Milwaukee Chamber of Commerce. The rest of us think of bratwurst, cheese curds, bowling, and a really odd Fonzi statue.

Milwaukee is also home to the apartment building where Dahmer committed his atrocities. While the building where Dahmer committed his horrific murders was torn down in 1992, the lot still sits empty today. They say if you listen closely on a moonless night, you could hear the distant cries of those who suffered within its walls.

But I'm pretty sure you can't.

Dahmer was born in the town of West Allis, Wisconsin. He grew increasingly withdrawn and uncommunicative between the ages of ten and fifteen. But so did I and I don't have a bunch of heads in my freezer as far as you know. He didn't have any real hobbies or friends and spent much of his time biking around his neighborhood looking for dead animals. When he found them, he'd often dissect them. Once, he put a dog's head on a stake and even showed it to a friend as a practical joke.

Oh my, what a knee slapper that must have been.

Dahmer took his first life in the summer of 1978, a few weeks after he graduated high school. He picked up a hitchhiker named Steven Hicks. and brought him back to his house, ostensibly to drink beer, but the goal was to have sex. Hicks wasn't into that. When he tried to leave, Dahmer killed him by hitting him in the head with a ten-pound dumbbell, later saying he killed Hicks because "the guy wanted to leave and [he] didn't want him to." Dahmer buried the body in the backyard.

Dahmer attended Ohio State University but dropped out almost immediately without attending most of his classes. This probably had something to do with him being constantly drunk. He then joined the Army but was discharged because of the same boozehag vibe.

He was arrested twice for indecent exposure, in 1982 and 1986, for masturbating in public. Ahh, if only he just continued on with those innocent ways. He began working at a chocolate factory and found an apartment nearby. Shortly after he moved in, he was arrested for drugging and sexually fondling a thirteen-year-old boy. He was sentenced to five years' probation and one year in a work release camp and was forced to register as a sex offender.

In May 1990, he moved into the apartment that later became infamous: Apartment 213, 924 North 25th Street, Milwaukee.

In the early morning hours of May 27, 1991, a fourteen-year-old boy was found on the street near Dahmer's apartment, naked and seemingly under the influence of drugs.

He was also bleeding from his ass.

This understandably got the attention of three young women, who called 911. Dahmer arrived shortly after the call and tried to take the boy away, but the women made a scene until the police arrived. Dahmer told police officers that the boy was his nineteen-year-old boyfriend and that they'd had an argument while drinking, and everything was cool.

The officers turned him over to Dahmer despite the women's protests. They even brought the boy back to Dahmer's apartment. The officers later reported smelling something odd while inside the apartment but didn't bother to check it out. The smell was the body of Dahmer's previous victim, decomposing in the bedroom.

These two cops probably never made detective. I say that because they're dumb as fuck. Can you imagine going home every night and watching TV, knowing you literally brought a child back to Dahmer to be murdered and played with? They never verified the identity of the boy, or even worse, ran a background check on Dahmer, which would have shown he was a convicted child molester and on probation. Later that night, Dahmer killed and dismembered the boy and kept his skull as a souvenir.

By the summer of 1991, Dahmer was murdering an average of one person each week; most were gay men he met at bars. Dahmer was hopeful he could turn his victims into "zombies," who would serve him forever. He attempted to do so by drilling holes into his victims' skulls and injecting hydrochloric acid or boiling water into the frontal lobe area of their brains with a syringe.

Oddly enough, his zombie plan never worked. If it did, I wouldn't be writing about this now as I'd imagine the world would be run by King Jeff Dahmer and his army of zombie sex slaves.

Couldn't be worse than what's going on now.

Other residents of the apartment complex noticed a horrific stench coming from Dahmer's apartment as well as hearing thumps and bangs and what sounded like a power saw.

On July 22, 1991, Dahmer lured Tracy Edwards into his home to, you know, make him a bang zombie. Dahmer struggled with handcuffing Edwards, but Edwards punched Dahmer in the face, kicked him in the stomach, and ran through the streets, all with handcuffs still hanging from his wrist.

Police soon spotted him (how could they not?) and Edwards led them back to Dahmer's apartment. When one of the officers checked the bedroom, he saw photographs of dead and mangled bodies that he could tell were taken in the apartment and called out for his partner to arrest Dahmer. He tried to get away (really?) but was quickly subdued.

When the officers opened the refrigerator, they found a human head. Further searching of the apartment revealed three more severed heads, severed hands and penises, and more human remains in his refrigerator. Seven skulls were found in the apartment in all.

The Court found Dahmer sane (really?), guilty on fifteen counts of murder and sentenced him to fifteen life terms, totaling 957 years in prison. Dahmer was severely beaten by fellow inmate Christopher Scarver with a metal bar from the prison gym and died while incarcerated. Scarver claimed, "God told him to do it."

While in Milwaukee, check out the Miller Brewery Tour. Here you'll tour the 170-year-old factory and discover that living the "high life" involves drinking cheap swill in an outdoor beer garden with tourists from Minnesota.

JOHNNY TREVISANI WITH BRIAN WHITNEY

PLAINFIELD, WISCONSIN

Ed Gein—aka the Plainfield Ghoul
Kills: 2+
Span of Activity:1944 to 1957

A few hours south of Milwaukee is Plainfield, Wisconsin. The area was settled in 1840, where a dude from Plainfield, Vermont, named the town and started giving away free lots. Almost two hundred years later, there's nothing to do in Plainfield but hunt, watch the Packers, and get drunk. Which is pretty much all people from Wisconsin want to do anyway.

Ed Gein had other kicks.

Gein, aka the Plainfield Ghoul, was born in La Crosse County, Wisconsin. His parents eventually purchased a farm in Plainfield. The family moved to the farm to prevent outsiders from influencing their sons, which was, in retrospect, a shitty idea. He needed some outside influences. For real.

Gein left the farm only to go to school. His mother preached to her boys about how immoral the world was and that all women except her were nothing but whores. While I wasn't alive at this time, after doing research, I don't believe this to be true.

Gein was awkward as a child, often laughing to himself for no reason. His awkwardness didn't matter a whole lot as his mother didn't allow him to have friends anyway.

Gein's father died in 1940 of heart failure. In 1944, a brush fire occurred near the farm; Gein and his brother went to try to put it out. Later, Gein reported to the police that his brother was missing. They organized a search party and Gein led them directly to his missing brother, who lay dead with bruises on his head. The whole "My brother is missing—oh, there's his body!" vibe caused many investigators to believe Gein killed his sibling but he was never charged.

After his brother's death, Gein lived alone with his mother, who died on December 29, 1945, after which Gein lived on the farm alone.

This part of Gein's life was party time.

In 1957, Plainfield hardware store owner Bernice Worden disappeared. Gein was known to be the last person who was in the store before she vanished so the cops decided to pay ol' Ed a visit.

When police searched Gein's property, they found Worden's decapitated body in a shed, hung upside down. Her torso was "dressed" like a deer.

After searching the house, police found:

- Four noses
- Human bones and fragments
- Nine masks of human skin
- Bowls made from human skulls
- Ten female heads with the tops sawn off
- Human skin covering several chairs
- The head of a woman named Mary Hogan in a paper bag
- Bernice Worden's head in a burlap sack
- Nine vulvas in a shoe box
- Skulls on his bedposts
- Organs in the refrigerator
- A pair of lips on a drawstring for a window shade
- A belt made from human female nipples
- A lampshade made from the skin of a human face

Gein told investigators that over the years, he'd gone to graveyards dozens of times to exhume recently buried female bodies. He then brought the bodies home, where he tanned their skins and made his trophies. Gein denied having sex with the bodies he exhumed because "they smelled too bad." See? He's not that odd after all.

Gein also admitted to the shooting death of Hogan.

On November 21, 1957, Gein was arraigned on one count of first-degree murder in Waushara County Court, where he entered a plea of not guilty because of insanity. Found mentally incompetent and thus unfit to stand trial, Gein was sent to the Central State Hospital for the Criminally Insane. On July 26, 1984, Gein died of respiratory and heart failure due to cancer.

Before you leave Plainfield, check out the Annual Petenwell Palooza Ice Fisheree & Raffle in January at the Lure Bar & Grill. If you've never checked out an indoor ice fishing tournament, this is your chance. The top cash prize for adults is $1,500, and there are a lot of other prizes too, like a Coleman inflatable hot tub. The meat raffle is at one p.m.

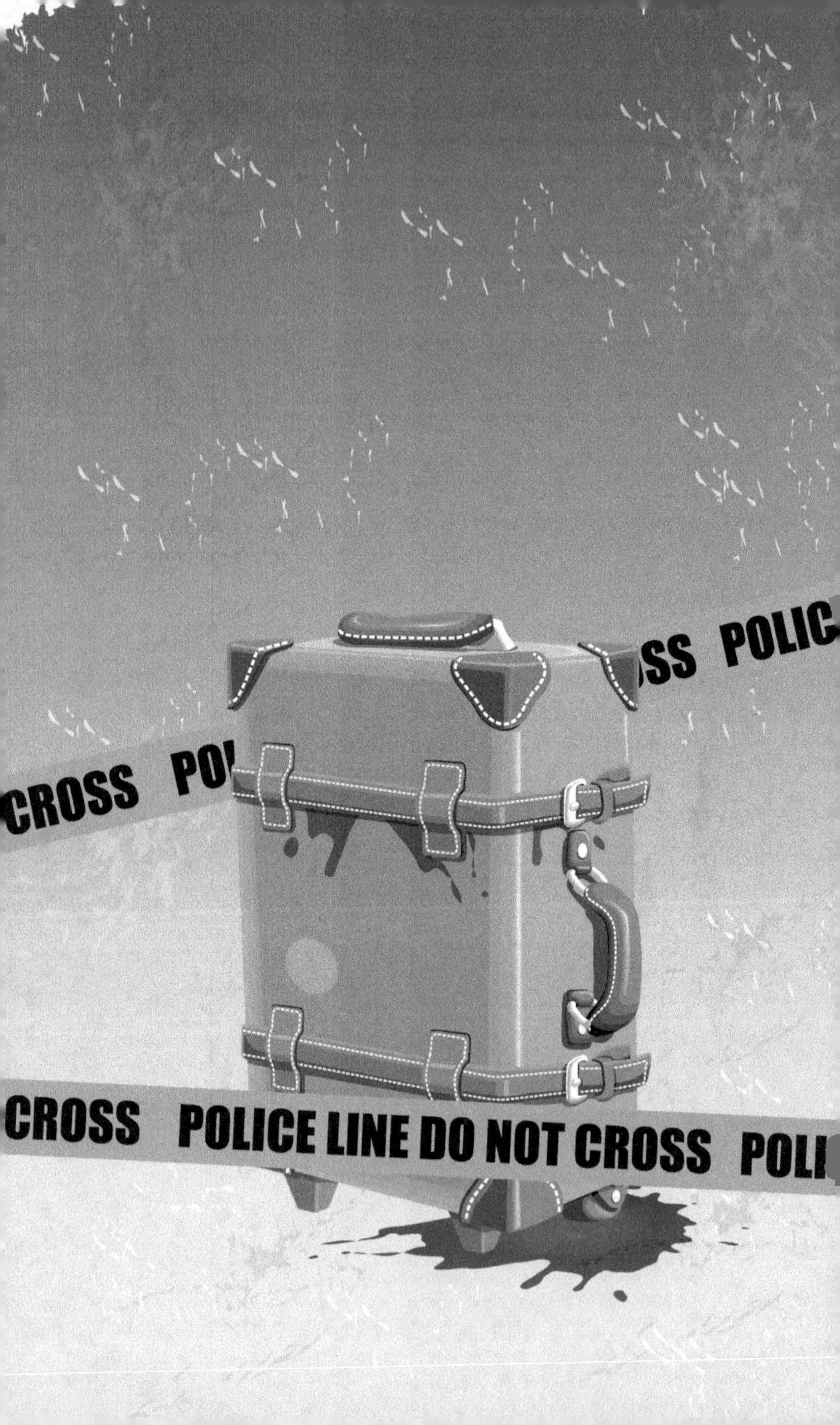

SS POLIC
CROSS PO
CROSS POLICE LINE DO NOT CROSS POLI

THE PLAINS

The Great Plains is a vast, flat, and grassy region that stretches across parts of the United States and Canada. In the nineteenth century, Americans flocked to the Midwest with the promise of free land to farm and hopes for a better future. Sadly, for the most part, their future sucked.

The Great Plains has been used for cattle ranching and agriculture since the nineteenth century. But things aren't always placid in the Plains, often called Tornado Alley; the area experiences the most tornadoes in the world.

The states in the Great Plains are...

Minnesota, the place you want to go if you're looking to discuss crock pots while looking out at the snow from your friend's cabin on the lake. Just don't overstay your welcome, because while Minnesotans are nice, they sure aren't kind.

Iowa is the place to be if you're into not having any access to the ocean, big cities, or any semblance of culture. Then there is Missouri, the home of harsh winters, blistering summers, crippling poverty, a lack of reproductive rights, and a brutal crime rate.

Then comes **Kansas**, a state I would think is godawful for a myriad of reasons, except my friend Shane lives there and he's usually right about a bunch of things. Once gone from Kansas, you can visit Nebraska. Some say the best thing to come out of Nebraska is I-80. It's a state where being in Tornado Alley and having a high crime rate are offset only by a complete lack of nightlife and the possibility of going to jail for possessing edibles.

North Dakota is a fine place for those who don't mind isolation and a lack of culture. They don't call it the Badlands for nothing. **South Dakota** has not one single serial killer I could find who did most of his work in that state. This stands to reason as it supports my theory: South Dakota doesn't actually exist.

There's some odd stuff in the Plains.

Some say the Leavenworth Local Hotel in Kansas is haunted by a little girl ghost and a former nun, and there are more UFO sightings in this region than one could shake a stick at.

However, like the rest of the regions in this book, what should concern you most while traveling the Plains is Man.

SAINT PAUL, MINNESOTA

Paul Stephani—aka the Weepy-Voiced Killer

Kills: 3

Span of Activity: December 1980 to August 1982

Fun Fact: Stephani asked for a photo of his mother's burial headstone in exchange for his confessions to the murders

One of oldest cities in Minnesota is Saint Paul, known for its historic neighborhoods, landmarks, and fun attractions. While here, check out the Cathedral of Saint Paul, a fine example of Beaux-Arts architecture. Then perhaps hit Summit Avenue, home to the longest stretch of Victorian-era homes in the United States. Saint Paul has the distinction of being a fairly large city that is perhaps best known for shitty winters, potholes large enough to lose a small dog in, and a bunch of people who get beer money by stealing copper wire.

Paul Stephani was born in 1944, the second of ten children. His mother remarried when he was three years old. His stepfather was a bit of a jerk; he was said to beat Stephani and his sibling, sometimes throwing them down the stairs for good measure.

Stephani married as a young man and had a daughter, but the couple soon divorced. He bounced from job to job, as many sociopaths tend to do. He worked as a janitor at Malberg Manufacturing Company; the body of his first victim was found near this job site.

In 1980, things started coming off the rails. One night, Stephani severely beat a woman in Saint Paul. He later called police to report the attack and told them where the victim was located. Is there anything more adorable than a serial killer with a conscience? I think not.

During the summer of 1981, he murdered eighteen-year-old

Kimberly Compton. After her death, he called police, saying, "God damn, will you find me? I just stabbed somebody with an ice pick. I can't stop myself. I keep killing somebody." He called the police numerous times after this initial call, speaking in a whimpering, high-pitched voice about how bad he felt about slaughtering a teenage girl. Which is nice, I suppose, but not as nice as not killing her at all. Man up, for crying out loud! Because of these pathetic phone calls, he became known as the Weepy-Voice Killer.

Shortly afterwards, he killed Kathleen Greening, who was found dead in her home, drowned in a bathtub. His last victim was Barbara Simons, whom he stabbed to death after they went home together from a bar. The Weepy-Voiced Killer again called police and apologized. What a polite young man.

Stephani picked up a sex worker, Denise Williams, in 1982 in Minneapolis. Once he had her in his vehicle, he stabbed her fifteen times with a screwdriver, but she fought back and was able to hit him on the head with a bottle. The commotion caused a witness to come running, and Stephani fled the scene. The combination of the witness being able to identify Stephani and the fact he sought medical attention after this attack, as he was bleeding badly, caused him to be arrested. Police were later able to connect Stephani to Simons' murder.

Stephani was convicted of the Simons murder and of the attempted murder of Williams. He was sentenced to fifty-eight years. He later confessed to three other murders, presumably crying and apologizing all the while. He died in prison in 1998.

On the way out of St. Paul, check out the Minnesota State Fair. Known as the Great Minnesota Get-Together, two million people show up each year to check out livestock, agriculture, horse, art, talent, and creative activities competitions. Don't forget to try the cheese curds when you're there.

DUBUQUE, IOWA

Mary Clement
Kills: 5
Span of Activity: 1880 to 1885

Welcome to Dubuque. A place where residents bond by being evenly divided between their distrust of non-locals and minorities. Some in Dubuque used to complain about the cost of living in an area with not a damn thing to do when IBM was located here. After IBM left, those same people can comfortably afford rent, they just have to be worried about trash blowing down the street and getting stabbed.

Mary Clement was born in Luxemburg. She, her parents, and four sisters immigrated to the United States in 1871. She was pretty as a child, but because of a spinal defect, only had a partial ability to move her legs and feet. Apparently, that got in her head a little. What's the point of being pretty if you have weird feet?

In 1880, her sister Annie began convulsing and died. Doctors thought it was because she ate too much before going to bed. I have to tell you, if that's the truth, I would have died a long time ago. Over the next few years, her parents and another sister died in the same manner.

Clement then moved in with her sister and her husband, Michael, and their two children. I mean, she kind of had to, 'cause she killed her whole family and all. Every time she cooked for her sister, brother-in-law, and their children, all of them got violently sick. Michael soon became suspicious because Mary would never eat the meals she made.

Seriously? She moved in because four people died for "no reason" and now his whole family is sick every time she cooks, and he's "suspicious"? This dude is not Columbo, but I'll refrain from making fun of him further as it's apparent he was the only one in this family who could think his way out of a paper bag.

He soon found some grayish-colored powder around the home and brought it to law enforcement to be analyzed. It turned out to be arsenic, and Mary was arrested.

Mary Clement was sentenced to a year in jail as she wasn't charged for the murders, just the attempted poisoning. She later wrote a letter confessing her crimes. Upon her release, she moved to Los Angeles and became a servant for a wealthy family. She never discussed her crimes and was known as a nice woman who was fond of hats. She died at eighty-one.

Before leaving town, check out Paul's Tavern, a local favorite. Known for their burgers and big game trophies, this tavern is home to a small menu and big history of good food. Nothing beats eating a one-pound cheeseburger while being surrounded by dead animals.

Nothing.

MOORESVILLE, MISSOURI

Ray Copeland
Kills: 5-12
Span of Activity: 1986 to 1989

West of Streamwood sits Mooresville, Missouri. You can stroll through their historic downtown square, hit the links on one of their golf courses, hunt for that antique treasure through dozens of magnificent shops, or have some outdoor fun with the family at one of their many parks. While doing so, you can ruminate on area issues like low life expectancies, high poverty rates, and limited access to healthcare and essential services. But residents can take solace at the low crime rates, mostly because no one in town has anything worth stealing.

There was crime here, once. Ray Copeland was born in Oklahoma in 1914. He grew up poor, as many did during the Great Depression. As a young man, he began a life of petty crime, stealing livestock and forging checks. Eventually, he was caught and spent a year in jail. After his release in 1940, he met Faye Wilson, and they were married soon afterward.

Ray was known not to be trusted, so no one would sell him cattle. He'd hook up with drifters and use them at auction to buy cattle for him, then the drifter would go on his way. The only problem was the checks he wrote to the drifter and for the cattle were always bad. After a while, he was sent back to jail.

When he was released, he changed up his plan a bit. One day in 1989, a former employee called the Crime Stoppers hotline to tell them Ray had tried to kill him. He also said he'd seen human bones on the farm. Police paid a visit to the Copeland

farm and found the bodies of three men in a barn. It remains unclear whether they were killed to keep them quiet about fraud they'd participated in or because Copeland murdered them to steal their possessions.

Obviously, Copeland had killed the men, but was Faye involved or was she a victim herself? The jury thought so as she was convicted of five counts of murder and sentenced to death. She was the oldest woman on death row when her sentence was commuted life without parole in 1999. She died of natural causes at the age of eighty-two in 2003.

Ray Copeland was sentenced to death. He died of natural causes on October 19, 1993.

Before you leave town, visit The Parcade. The Parcade was founded to eliminate weather variables and allow golfers to play any day they want. Indoor golf. What a wonderful world.

KANSAS CITY, MISSOURI

Terry Blair
Kills: 7+
Span of Activity:1982 and 2003 to 2004

From Mooresville, we head west to Kansas City, Missouri. Kansas City is known for its jazz clubs and barbecue. So if you like Count Basie and burnt ends, you can probably put up with the occasional violent crime, awful roads, and a lack of public transportation. Kansas City has all the big-city amenities yet still has a small-town feel—and by that, I mean people are unfriendly in a very polite way. Almost like they're doing you a favor by acting like an asshole.

Speaking of assholes, Terry Blair was the fourth eldest of ten siblings, born to a mother who suffered from mental illness.

Blair came from a lovely family.

Blair's mother shot and killed her common-law husband.

Blair's brother, Walter, killed sixteen-year-old Sandy Shannon during a robbery but the case was dropped after witnesses refused to testify. But he wasn't done. On August 19, 1979, Walter Blair abducted, then shot and killed twenty-one-year-old Katherine Jo Allen. Walter was convicted of murder, sentenced to death, and executed.

Blair's sister, Warnetta, was charged in the murder of James L. Bell, whose body was found after being stabbed thirty times. Warnetta testified against her husband in exchange for charges against her being dropped. She wasn't done either. She later killed her boyfriend because he threatened to cut off her supply of crack cocaine. Makes sense when you think about it.

But this story is about Terry.

In 1982, Terry Blair was found guilty of killing Angela Monroe, the mother of two of Blair's children. Blair was sentenced to twenty-five years' imprisonment and was released on parole after twenty-one years. According to some, he was pissed because she was making money as a sex worker. If that's true, I imagine what he was angry about was her keeping her money for herself.

In 2004, a year or so after Blair was released, a neighbor found two women's bodies in the garage of an abandoned home. An anonymous man called the police and said he'd killed the women and told them where to find another woman's body in an alley nearby. The same man called police again a few months later and told them there were a few bodies in the tall grass near a highway. He said he'd call again soon.

Blair was a suspect almost immediately. Not only was he on parole for murder but he matched the description of a man who'd been raping and assaulting women in the neighborhood. The police arrested him on a parole violation charge just to get him off the streets. On October 15, 2004, Terry Blair was charged with eight counts of first-degree murder, one count of first-degree assault, and three counts of forcible rape.

Judge O'Malley ruled Blair guilty on March 27, 2008, and he was sentenced to six life sentences with no possibility of parole. Blair died in prison in 2004.

Before you leave, you have to check out the shuttlecocks on the grounds of the Nelson-Atkins Museum of Art in Kansas City, Missouri. They're huge. Like, eighteen feet high or something.

Not kidding. They're *really* big. They're supposed to suggest a game of badminton was played by giants using the museum building as a net.

But come on. We're not *stupid*.

WICHITA, KANSAS

Dennis Rader—aka the BTK Killer
Kills: 12+
Span of Activity: January 1974 to
January 1981

A few hours southwest of Kansas City is Wichita, Kansas, known for its culture, history, and affordability. When it comes to cities, "affordability" is cool, but what makes a city affordable these days is being an awful place to live. It's also home to many attractions, including museums, a zoo, and the fabulous Wichita Art Museum. Wichita is known as the birthplace of Pizza Hut and White Castle.

It's also known as the home of the Wichita State Shockers, which has led to thousands of college students at sporting events making the universal sign for "one in the stink, two in the pink." Shh. Don't tell anyone.

Dennis Rader was born in Pittsburg, Kansas, on March 9, 1945. Both of his parents worked a lot, and Rader was alone often as a child, which obviously explains everything. As a side note to parents, if your kids turns out fucked up, it's because of you.

Rader had a dark passenger very early on, harboring fantasies from a very young age about torturing helpless women. As an adolescent, Rader began breaking into homes, stealing underwear, and spying on women. After graduating high school, he attended Kansas Wesleyan University but dropped out and joined the Air Force.

Rader married Paula Dietz, who obviously isn't that great at judging people. They eventually had two children. He began

working for a security alarm system company; many of the homes he serviced purchased an alarm because they were worried about the BTK killer. One can just imagine how excited this murderous oddball felt while installing burglar alarms to keep himself out.

Rader was a damn good guy. Just ask him! He was a member of Christ Lutheran Church in Wichita, and at one point was elected president of the church council. He was also a Cub Scout leader.

On January 15, 1974, four members of the Otero family were murdered in Wichita. The victims were Julia and Joseph Otero Sr., and their children, nine-year-old Joey and eleven-year-old Josie. When Rader first arrived at their home, Joseph said, "Is this a joke or something? My brother-in-law put you up to this?" After killing the parents and their young son, Rader led Josie down into the basement, where he hanged her with a noose from a pipe.

Over the next few years, Rader killed numerous women. In 1978, Rader sent a letter to a Wichita television station in which he took responsibility for the murders and ruminated about names he should be known by, one of which was BTK. He wrote, "How many do I have to kill, before I get a name in the paper or some national attention?"

What a pathetic loser, not only bashing through life taking lives and causing immense pain and sorrow, but he wants attention for it too. Nevertheless, the national attention this freakshow sought eventually came.

In 1985, he killed Marine Hedge. He took her body to Christ Lutheran Church, where he was the president of the church council, and photographed her body in all sorts of sexual poses.

In 1986, he strangled Vicki Lynn Wegerle to death at her house in Wichita. On January 18, 1991, he murdered Dolores

Davis, his final victim. Her body was discovered by a fifteen-year-old boy under a bridge on February 1, 1991.

Then he just stopped. The case went cold. But you know, Rader still needed attention and all.

In 2004, this pathetic child sent a letter to the *Wichita Eagle* containing photos of a victim and a copy of her driver's license. He then wrote numerous letters to police; in one, he asked if a floppy disk could be traced back to him if he used it to send them a message. Law enforcement publicly responded, saying it was untraceable.

Rader, who, after all this supervillain buildup, turned out to be an incredible dummy, sent in a letter on a floppy disk to the police. This is the same vibe as the drug dealers back in the day who believed asking a potential buyer, "Are you a cop?" meant the person had to tell you the truth.

They don't.

The disc had metadata on it that was traced to Rader's church. It turned out "Dennis" was the last person to modify the document. On February 25, 2005, Rader was arrested, bringing an end to his decades-long reign of terror.

Rader was charged with ten counts of first-degree murder. In June 2005, he pleaded guilty to all charges and talked in detail about each murder in court because he's that much of a loser.

On August 18, 2005, Dennis Rader was sentenced to ten consecutive life terms in prison with no possibility of parole for 175 years. He is currently incarcerated at the El Dorado Correctional Facility in Kansas. He is now in solitary confinement for his protection. You know, because he's a total prick.

Wichita can be pretty hot in the summer. If you need something to keep it out of your face, check out Hatman

Jack's. They've been proudly serving the public for over four decades. Why? Because they're passionate about finding the cowboy, outdoor, or period hat that fits you perfectly. Go get a hat, for crying out loud.

OGALLAH, KANSAS

Francis Nemechek
Kills: 5
Span of Activity: December 1974
to August 1976

Fun Fact: Nemechek played football in high school

Three hours northwest of Kansas City is Ogallah, an unincorporated community in Trego County and located roughly fourteen miles from Cedar Bluff State Park. Activities at the state park include hiking, biking, horseback riding, paddle sports, and beaches. Of course, living fourteen miles from a state park isn't all that much of a claim to fame. But if you don't mind a lack of jobs and services, social isolation, no entertainment options all while living surrounded by rednecks, this vibe might be for you.

Born on June 29, 1950, Francis Donald Nemechek was the second of three children. After high school, he got a job as a mechanic. Eventually, Nemechek married and had a son. He was well on his way to being a fine young man—until the marriage ended in divorce. Those close to Nemechek said he would flip right out if anyone mentioned his ex, which isn't all that surprising because that's what psychotic, controlling oddballs do.

In 1974, Nemechek was driving around in his truck on the highway near Ogallah when he saw two young women driving along in a red pickup truck. The occupants of the truck were nineteen-year-old Diane Lovette, her friend twenty-one-year-old Cheryl Young, and her three-year-old son, Guy. Nemechek took out a gun and shot out the tires of their truck, 'cause hey, why not? When they pulled over, he abducted them and took them to a farmhouse. He sexually assaulted

one woman, then shot them both. He left the Young boy, who later died of hypothermia because of the snow and freezing temps.

During the summer of 1974, Nemechek drove past a girl on a bicycle, then stopped his truck and exposed himself. According to Nemechek, the girl said, "You stupid bastard, you think you are funny?"

The thing is, Nemechek was a stupid bastard and was not funny, so her comments were apt. Still, Nemechek, who obviously lacked self-awareness, flipped right out. He forced her into his truck and raped her. Then he stabbed her to death and left her body in a wheat field.

On August 21, Nemechek abducted sixteen-year-old Paula Fabrizius. He drove her to a secluded area where he raped her and stabbed her to death.

A few days later, Nemechek was arrested at his job for the murder of Fabrizius, as he was the last person seen with her, and his fingerprints linked him to the crime scene. While searching his camper, they found photos he'd taken of the victims' bodies, as well as a blood-soaked carpet.

He was charged with the five murders and found guilty. He was sentenced to life in prison with a chance of parole after fifteen years. Nemechek's earliest possible parole date is July 26, 2027. He will be seventy-seven years old.

There aren't a whole lot of people who go to Ogallah, but if you do, check out the Ponderosa Tree Farm. They sell all sorts of stuff, including precut Christmas trees during the season. You might want to give them a ring and let them know you're coming.

LINCOLN, NEBRASKA

Charles Starkweather
Kills: 11
Span of Activity: November 1957 to January 1958

Northeast of Ogallah is Lincoln, home to a variety of top-rated attractions. Although I'm not entirely sure what they are. Lincoln is the kind of place where people say you'll make "plenty of friends in no time." You might, if you like sitting around doing the same old thing day after day. If you're a minority, expect to be stared at occasionally and fist-bumped often. Lincoln is the kind of place where if you aren't married by twenty-five, something is drastically wrong with you.

There was definitely something wrong with Charles Starkweather.

Starkweather was born in Lincoln, Nebraska, the fourth of seven children. His parents divorced on the grounds of extreme cruelty by Starkweather's father. Charles was born with a birth defect that caused his legs to be misshapen, and he said he was teased because of a speech impediment. At one point, Starkweather turned mean and started to be known for violent outbursts and picking on others.

In 1957, Starkweather went to a service station in Lincoln and got angry at Robert Colvert for refusing to sell him a stuffed animal on credit. He then stole one hundred dollars at gunpoint, drove Colvert to a remote area, and shot him to death. How many lives have been lost because of stuffed animals?

Too many.

On January 21, 1958, nineteen-year-old Starkweather went to the home of his fourteen-year-old girlfriend, Caril Ann Fugate; he killed her mother and stepfather, Velda and Marion Bartlett, and their two-year-old daughter, ostensibly because they told him to leave.

Fugate claimed she didn't know about the murders and said Starkweather told her that if she cooperated with him, her family would be safe; otherwise, they would be killed. The pair then went to the home of a seventy-year-old man and killed him with a shot to the head. Starkweather then killed two local teenagers who'd stopped to give the pair a ride after their car was stuck in the mud.

They then went to the home of Chester and Clara Ward, people who Starkweather knew were wealthy. The plan was to rob them. Neither was home, so Starkweather killed their maid and waited for them to arrive. When they arrived, he killed them too and stole some jewelry as well as their car.

The cops were on the lookout for the stolen vehicle, so the pair needed a new one. Starkweather killed a traveling salesman and took his car. As he tried to leave the scene, a sheriff's deputy arrived. Fugate ran towards him, yelling, "It's Starkweather! He's going to kill me!"

To be clear, Starkweather claimed Fugate participated in each of these crimes, while she said she most certainly did not. The truth remains a mystery.

Starkweather drove away in great haste, but after a brief car chase, he surrendered, like the tough guy he was.

Starkweather testified against Fugate at her trial, saying that she was a willing participant. Fugate maintained that she was a hostage because he threatened to kill her family and she didn't know they were already dead.

Starkweather was convicted and sentenced to death. He was executed in the electric chair at the Nebraska State Penitentiary. Fugate is the youngest woman tried and convicted of first-degree murder when she was convicted as an accomplice and received a life sentence on November 21, 1958. She was paroled in June 1976 and moved to Michigan. She's still alive today.

Before leaving Lincoln, check out the Museum of American Speed, a non-profit museum dedicated to preserving and displaying artifacts of American automotive history. The museum was established by Speedway Motors founder "Speedy" Bill Smith and his wife Joyce as a repository for a collection of automobilia amassed over sixty years.

NIAGARA, NORTH DAKOTA

Eugene Butler—aka the Great Plains Butcher
Kills: 8
Span of Activity:1900 to 1906

Eugene Butler was born in Royalton, New York, in 1849. He moved to North Dakota around 1882 and purchased a 480-acre farm in Niagara. He never married and lived as a recluse. He did his best to avoid people and only went out if he needed to. In the summer, he'd hire farmhands to help.

Butler began showing signs of mental illness immediately after moving to town and was known to hallucinate. On top of that, he began riding around on his horse at night, screaming at the top of his lungs. If you're going to have hallucinations, for the love of God, keep them to yourself. He was soon admitted to the North Dakota State Hospital, which was basically a mental asylum. While there, he talked a lot about invisible people coming after him but didn't show any violent tendencies. In fact, he was a favorite of the staff.

He died while still at the asylum and his estate was divided up between his relatives.

Two years after Butler's death, workmen went to the farm to begin renovating the home. One workman found numerous human skeletons buried under the house; all of them had their skulls crushed. All of them were young men, almost certainly vagrants whom Butler hired as farmhands. Many suspect he killed the men because he was afraid they were going to steal his money, but that seems a little mundane to me. Because, you know, the dude was batshit crazy.

There are only forty-six people who live in Niagara, so let's go to nearby Grand Forks and check out the Half Brothers Brewing Company. There isn't anything to do in Grand Forks either, but at Half Brothers Brewing, one can get drunk.

SOUTHWEST

The Southwest is an unholy cocktail of desert heat, cowboy lawlessness, and too much damn space. Out here, the highways stretch into the abyss, dust devils swirl like lost souls, and neon-lit truck stops glow like cheap invitations to doom. It's the kind of place where you can vanish without a trace— where the rattlesnakes aren't the deadliest things slithering in the night.

But beneath the sun-scorched landscapes of Arizona, New Mexico, Oklahoma, and Texas, a darker breed of predator has always lurked, stalking the open roads and back alleys like shadows with a pulse. Some of the most twisted minds in American history carved their bloody legacies into these lands—ghosts of violence still lingering in the dry air.

Arizona
Mark Goudeau, the Baseline Killer—A Phoenix nightmare in the mid-2000s, Goudeau terrorized the city with nine murders, brutal rapes, and a sadistic flair for unpredictability. He stalked the streets in disguise, blending into the hazy mirage of the scorching Arizona summer, striking when his victims least expected.

New Mexico
David Parker Ray, the Toy Box Killer—If Hell had an address, it might've been a soundproof trailer in Elephant Butte, where Ray spent years abducting, torturing, and murdering women in ways so sick even Satan would take notes. He had a dungeon full of whips, chains, and a chilling recorded tape explaining in grim detail what his victims were about to endure. Officially,

no bodies were found—but authorities estimate he killed up to sixty women, maybe more.

Oklahoma

Nannie Doss, the Lonely Hearts Killer—Oklahoma's most polite serial killer, Doss poisoned her husbands, children, and other relatives with a smile on her face and a twinkle in her eye. She laughed through her confession, a twisted homemaker who found joy in watching her loved ones drop dead from arsenic-laced meals.

Texas

Texas is a serial killer's wet dream—long highways, empty landscapes, corrupt small-town sheriffs, and enough weirdness to make your brain melt faster than a Blue Bell ice cream cone on a Corpus Christi sidewalk.

Dean Corll, the Candy Man—Along with his teenage accomplices, Corll lured young boys to their deaths in the 1970s, torturing and murdering at least twenty-eight victims in his twisted Houston house of horrors. He bribed them with candy. Let that sink in.

The Texas Killing Fields—A stretch of land along I-45 between Houston and Galveston, where dozens of women have vanished or been found dead since the 1970s. Multiple killers? One man? The Devil himself? No one knows. But if you're driving through and see a hitchhiker, keep driving.

PHOENIX, ARIZONA

Mark Goudeau—aka the Baseline
Killer
Kills: 9
Span of Activity: August 2005 to
June 2006

Fun Fact: His wife stood by him throughout his trial, insisting he was innocent

Welcome to Phoenix, Arizona—a city built on asphalt, mirages, and the bad decisions of people who thought living in a literal oven was a good idea. The sun here isn't just hot; it's a merciless god, burning everything in sight. You can fry an egg on the sidewalk, melt the soles off your shoes, and hallucinate lizard people after two margaritas and heatstroke.

Phoenix is America's most dangerous suburb. A sprawling, never-ending grid of stucco houses, strip malls, and angry retirees who drive like they've got nothing to lose. But beneath its beige, sun-blasted exterior, there's something truly weird bubbling under the surface. A strange energy that attracts outlaws, wanderers, and the kind of people who don't fit anywhere else.

If you're brave (or stupid) enough to explore, here's your degenerate's guide to the Valley of the Sun.

Tucked away in the foothills of South Mountain, surrounded by cacti and dust, is a castle built out of trash. This deranged middle finger of architecture was constructed in the 1930s by a man named Boyce Luther Gulley, who fled to the desert after being diagnosed with tuberculosis. Instead of seeking medical treatment like a rational human, he decided to build a castle out of junk—everything from car parts to telephone poles to discarded railroad tracks.

The result? A three-thousand-square-foot Frankenstein's monster of a home, complete with secret passageways, dusty old furniture, and a room designed for a princess who never arrived. Gulley's daughter, Mary Lou, lived there for years, giving tours to confused tourists who stumbled in expecting a medieval fortress but instead found a madman's tribute to hoarding.

Maybe Mark Goudeau spent some time in that house of trash—you never know.

If you've ever wondered what happens when a person takes all their worst instincts, blends them with a complete lack of self-control, and then marinates the whole thing in Phoenix heat, I present to you Mark Goudeau.

Known as the Baseline Killer, Goudeau terrorized Phoenix between August 2005 and June 2006, proving that even in a city where it's too hot to function, people will still find time for violent crime. His crimes were so varied (robbery, rape, and murder) that the police had a hard time pinning down a pattern—aside from the fact that he dressed like a homeless man with a baseball cap and would occasionally pose as a handyman. Because nothing screams "trust me!" like a sweaty man in a utility vest standing in a gas station parking lot.

Before his reign of terror, Goudeau was a construction worker with a criminal past and a seemingly normal life. One of those guys who probably made weird small talk in the break room, but nothing that would make you immediately cross the street to avoid him. That is, until he decided to spend his nights robbing convenience stores, assaulting women, and ultimately killing nine people. As if Phoenix didn't have enough problems already.

Once you finish meandering around Mr. Goudeau's favorite places to murder, you may need a drink. However, Phoenix doesn't do classy drinking. It's too hot, too angry, and too full

of transplanted Midwesterners who just want cheap beer and air conditioning. If you're looking for a place that feels like it's been preserved in alcohol-soaked amber since 1947, then you need to stumble into the Bikini Lounge.

This dark, windowless Tiki dive is where hipsters, drunks, and old-school degenerates come together in a glorious, sweaty mess. The drinks are strong enough to give you heatstroke indoors, the jukebox is unpredictable, and the regulars look like they've been here since Bugs Bunny took a left turn at Albuquerque.

ELEPHANT BUTTE, NEW MEXICO

David Parker Ray—aka the Toy
Box Killer
Victims: 0 to 60
Span of Activity: 1957 to 1999

Elephant Butte, New Mexico, is a place where the desert meets the lake and sanity is optional. A godforsaken outpost of fishermen, sun-scorched retirees, and the occasional drifter looking to escape something—be it the law, an ex-wife, or their own crippling self-awareness. The air is thick with heat, the roads are cracked, and everything smells like a mix of motor oil, fried food, and evaporated lake water. Welcome.

If you have even the faintest love for water and aren't afraid of what might be lurking in the depths, Elephant Butte Lake is your primary destination. It's the largest body of water in New Mexico, which is a bit like saying you've found the tallest hill in Kansas—but let's not split hairs. Here, you can rent a boat, fish for catfish the size of small dogs, or just float under the sun while watching old-timers on pontoons slowly drink themselves into a stupor. The lake has its own mythology: ghost stories of drowned mobsters, submerged towns, and rumors of prehistoric creatures that have adapted to nuclear waste. Whether any of that is true doesn't matter. This is a place where stories become reality if you merely drink enough.

Just a short drive away, in the town formerly known as Hot Springs (until a radio contest convinced them to rename it after a game show), you'll find the legendary geothermal baths. It's the kind of place that smells vaguely of sulfur and desperation, where people soak themselves in ancient waters in an attempt to heal whatever modern medicine has failed to fix. Rumors abound that these hot springs have mystical properties—some say they grant visions, others claim they dissolve all the bad decisions you've made. The clientele is an odd mix of hippies, conspiracy theorists, and old cowboys who never left. If you go, bring an open mind and a towel you don't care about.

David Parker Ray was, for lack of a better term, the worst neighbor you could possibly have. Not because he played his music too loudly or borrowed your lawnmower without returning it, but because he kept a soundproof trailer in his backyard—a twisted little hobby space he referred to as his "toy box." And inside? Well, let's just say it wasn't filled with action figures or Lincoln Logs.

Born in 1939 in Belen, New Mexico, Ray had what true crime enthusiasts and lazy psychologists might call a "troubled childhood." His father was an abusive drinker who popped in and out of his life, leaving him in the hands of his equally charming grandfather. One might imagine young David Parker Ray spending his days collecting baseball cards, or setting ants on fire with a magnifying glass—standard training for the psychologically askew. But no, Ray's real awakening came when he discovered sadomasochistic pornography, a discovery that apparently set him on a lifelong mission to ensure that no woman ever had a peaceful road trip through the Southwest again.

His career as a mechanic seemed to be going fine—at least, fine for a man who spent his free time constructing an elaborate torture chamber filled with pulleys, whips, and a voice recording so vile it would make a seasoned FBI profiler reconsider their career choices. The authorities believe he may have killed as many as sixty women, but Ray, ever the secretive handyman, never admitted to a single murder. As evidence that Ray wouldn't win Father of the Year, his daughter contacted the FBI to inform them about his odd hobbies. The FBI, in keeping with their we-know-better attitude, dismissed her allegations as "too vague." Well done, FBI! His trial, a drawn-out mess of mistrials, witnesses, and small-town drama, eventually landed him a 224-year prison sentence. It would have been a fitting end, but in a final act of audacity, he died of a heart attack in 2002 before serving a single day of it.

You're going to need a drink—several, actually. And that means heading to Bigfoot's Bar & Grill, the best and worst place to drown your sorrows in Elephant Butte. No one's quite sure how it got its name, but the walls are lined with blurry photos of alleged Bigfoot sightings, including a particularly unsettling one that might just be a very hairy local. The beer is cold, the whiskey is cheap, and the bartender looks like she could break your fingers if you get out of line. It's the kind of place where bikers and fishermen coexist in a fragile peace, bonded by their shared love of alcohol and bad decisions. Live music sometimes graces the corner stage—usually a guy named "Rooster" who only knows three songs but plays them with the passion of a man who lost everything in a poker game.

TULSA, OKLAHOMA

Nannie Doss—aka the Lonely Hearts Killer
Kills: 11
Span of Activity: August 1923 to October 1954

Welcome to Tulsa, Oklahoma—the psychedelic armpit of the Midwest. A place where Route 66 ghosts still hitchhike through oil-slicked dreams, where the barbecue is smoked with equal parts hickory and sin, and the locals smile like they know something you don't—and they do. Jesus lives here, but so does the Devil, and they share a one-bedroom off Admiral Boulevard.

First stop: the Center of the Universe.

This is not a metaphor. This is a concrete circle in downtown Tulsa where the laws of physics take a coffee break. Stand in the middle and speak. You'll hear your own voice echo like the gods are mocking you. Step outside the circle and the magic dies. No one knows why. Locals shrug and mutter about "ley lines" or "tornado acoustics."

Bring the hard stuff. You'll need it to understand the metaphysical implications.

And then there's Nannie Doss.

Nannie Doss, born Nancy Hazel in 1905 in Blue Mountain, Alabama, was the sort of woman who would crochet you a potholder while slowly stirring arsenic into your banana pudding. People called her "the Giggling Granny," which sounds whimsical until you learn she giggled during interrogations. It's

one thing to laugh at a funeral because someone tripped into the casket; it's another to laugh because you put them there.

Her origin story is something out of a Southern gothic horror novel: strict father, limited education, a head injury on a train (of course), and a tendency to disappear into romance magazines the way most girls her age disappeared into prayer or embroidery. While other young women dreamed of chivalry and courtship, Nannie was clipping coupons for arsenic and fantasizing about men who wouldn't make it past dessert.

She married five times. This would be impressive if she weren't also her own divorce attorney, judge, and mortician.

The first husband was a philanderer. The second was a drunk. The third—well, honestly, I lost track. By the fourth, you start to think, *Maybe it's not them. Maybe it's you, Nannie.* Still, it's hard not to admire her commitment. She took marriage seriously—just not necessarily the person she married.

After the fourth or fifth death, one of the husbands was found with symptoms so suspicious even the 1950's police, a group not known for their deductive reasoning, raised an eyebrow. Autopsy! Arsenic! Scandal!

When they finally arrested her, she confessed freely and cheerfully, like sharing a recipe at a church potluck. She claimed she sought the perfect man—someone sweet, loving, and faithful. She never found him, though she killed a few contenders along the way. I suppose it's hard to find a soulmate when you keep poisoning them with pie. In the end, she killed four husbands, two children, a sister, her mother, two grandsons, and a mother-in-law. I guess she kept it in the family.

Before you leave Tulsa, make sure you stop by the Mercury Lounge. It's a smoky sanctuary of regret and redemption, lit by neon and bad decisions.

Inside: A bar older than most religions. A jukebox that only plays outlaw country and songs about truck crashes. Bartenders who've seen things, *real* things, and will still pour you a double if you don't stare too long into the eyes and soul of the taxidermied raccoon by the bathroom.

Order the cheapest beer. Light a cigarette if you dare. Then sit back and listen to the guy next to you explain how he once  wrestled a goat in Broken Arrow for a bag of weed and a ride to prison. He's not lying.

CROSS POLICE LINE DO NOT CROSS POLICE
POLIC
CROSS POLICE LINE DO NOT CROSS
CROSS POLICE LINE DO NOT CROSS

HOUSTON, TEXAS

Dean Corll—aka the Candy Man
Kills: 28+
Span of Activity: September 1970
to August 1973

Fun Fact: Corll played the trombone in high school

Tie some longhorns onto the front of your car and head south to Houston. It's a place where humidity clings to your skin like guilt, and the skyline looks like a chrome hallucination dreamt up by a schizophrenic oil baron. God didn't make Houston—ExxonMobil did, and they did it with bad acid and bulldozers.

Sure, the air is thick with the wonderful aroma of barbecue smoke. But it's also thick with refinery fumes and the distant echo of televangelists speaking in tongues. This is a city that was never meant to be walked; it was meant to be driven, preferably in a '76 Cadillac with expired tags, two pit bulls, and a trunk full of (illegal) fireworks.

Houston is a feverish sprawl—a concrete octopus fueled by diesel and Whataburger. Don't look for logic. Don't expect charm. Just surrender. It will break you and then hand you a breakfast taco and ask you to stay a while.

The people here are too tired to judge and too sweaty to care. It's the kind of place where you can live ten lives in one week, then disappear into the bayou with a six-pack and a vague sense of purpose.

This travel guide wouldn't be complete without a visit to a stop at the National Museum of Funeral History. Nestled somewhere between a Taco Cabana and a strip mall that time forgot, the National Museum of Funeral History is where you go when you've seen too much—or not enough.

This place is a shrine to the final ride: embalming tools, vintage hearses, papal funerary exhibits, and JFK's eternal flame recreated in miniature. It's like Disneyland for the morbidly curious. One minute you're learning about Egyptian mummification and the next, you're standing in front of a glittering coffin shaped like a chicken leg.

No one talks above a whisper. The air smells like carpet cleaner and existential dread. Go early. Bring bourbon. Leave with a profound respect for morticians and a creeping fear of caskets with velvet interiors.

And then there's Dean Corll. Man. This guy.

Born in 1939 in Indiana—because, of course, he was—Corll was a quiet, polite boy. He played the trombone and was reportedly "nice to his mother."

The family moved to Texas, which is always where things get dicey. They opened a candy factory—Corll Candy Company—which sounds adorable until you realize the guy running it looked like the assistant manager of a funeral home and had all the emotional warmth of a refrigerator gasket. But kids liked him. He gave out free candy. He smiled a lot. And as we know from decades of after-school specials, anyone giving out free candy is probably up to something grim.

And he was.

After high school, Corll was drafted into the United States Army but only served ten months, getting a hardship discharge for claiming he was needed to run his family's candy business. It was during his time in the Army that he disclosed his homosexual tendencies. Due to the times, one can assume the Army was as eager to get rid of him as much as he wanted to get back to the candy business.

Corll returned to Houston Heights and resumed his position as vice president of Corll Candy Company. When the company relocated to 22nd Street, directly across the street from Helms Elementary School, Corll was known to give free candy to local children, in particular teenage boys. The kids called him Candy Man and the Pied Piper.

He eventually got bored of running the candy shop (who doesn't?) and pivoted to luring young boys into his home with the help of a couple of teenage accomplices. Now, I don't know how your teenage years went, but mine involved orthodontics and a great deal of *not* helping middle-aged men with murder. But these boys—Elmer Wayne Henley and David Brooks— were, shall we say, unusually impressionable. Instead of doing what normal teenagers do—drinking Mad Dog 20/20 and writing bad poetry—they helped Dean Corll abduct, torture, and kill at least twenty-nine teenagers and young men.

Corll's murder room (and yes, there was a murder room because he was thorough) was covered in plastic and filled with handcuffs, boards, and... well, you get the picture. It was the kind of place where a Roomba would immediately self-destruct out of despair.

Eventually, Henley—perhaps after a long moment of clarity, or because Corll told him to turn down his music—snapped and shot Corll dead in his living room. "I can't go on," he reportedly said, as if he were quitting a book club and not confessing to the most grotesque series of killings in Houston history.

While on your journey, Corll buried bodies in one of four places: Southwest Houston, a beach on the Bolivar Peninsula, a woodland near Lake Sam Rayburn, or a beach in Jefferson County.

Before you leave Houston, stop by the West Alabama Ice House.

No walls. Just picnic tables, stray dogs, and cold beer in buckets. You sit outside and watch the city's weirdest creatures pass by—cowboys on fixies, crypto bros in bolo ties, drunk professors quoting Kant. If the world ends, this place will still be open, slinging Lone Stars and charging five bucks for a game of cornhole with a guy named Blade.

They don't serve food, but a taco truck lurks nearby like a greasy angel of mercy. Tip well. And don't ask for a cocktail unless you want to be politely escorted to your car by a man wearing flip-flops and a gun.

INTERSTATE 45

The Texas Killing Fields
Kills: 30+
Span of Activity: June 1971 to
October 2006

This stretch of asphalt—from Houston to Galveston—isn't a road; it's a manifestation of evil, a blacktop artery pulsing with dead dreams, broken glass, and the lingering stink of body spray and despair. They call it the Texas Killing Fields, and brother, they're not being poetic. The bones are real. The ghosts don't lie.

It started in the early 1970s. Girls gone missing. Bodies dumped in the brush off the highway—open fields, muddy ditches, places God doesn't bother looking anymore.

The FBI has a term for it: a dumping ground.

Locals just call it "that place you don't go after dark."

From League City to Texas City to the motels that offer hourly rates and spiritual decline, the I-45 corridor has hosted at least thirty unsolved murders, mostly women, mostly young, mostly discarded like fast-food wrappers tossed from a moving car. This probably isn't one killer. It's probably a network of human filth, an open wound where the American Dream rotates in the sun.

And no one seems particularly eager to clean it up.

As you attempt this drive, know that it's flat down here. Unsettlingly flat. The kind of place where the horizon looks like a lie and your radio starts picking up gospel stations even when it's off.

Oil refineries cough up smoke like diseased lungs. Billboards alternate between Jesus and strip clubs. And beneath it all—the fields. Acres of reeds and marshland, obscuring stories no one wants to hear.

You can still see crosses marking where they found bodies. Some are official. Others are homemade: rebar and duct tape, a child's bracelet looped around a weathered stake. They never caught the guy. Or maybe they did and he was just one of many.

I-45 is the artery of entropy, a place where America's darkest impulses merge with the convenience of a nearby exit ramp.

Stay off the shoulder.

Keep your windows up.

Don't stop for hitchhikers—especially the ones who smile too much.

And if you ever feel something watching you from the fields, don't look—It already knows your name.

God bless Texas.

But not this part. Never this part.

If you're driving down I-45 in Texas, you might want to stop at Love's Travel Stop, in large part because if you run out of gas on the highway, you may want to visit a glory hole too. Not necessarily in that order. At Love's, the tacos are made fresh daily.

JOHNNY TREVISANI with BRIAN WHITNEY

ROCKY MOUNTAINS

The Rocky Mountain region is a beautiful place known for its stunning natural beauty, towering peaks, diverse wildlife, the Continental Divide, as well as the Rocky Mountain National Park and Glacier National Park. The entire area features diverse ecosystems and abundant wildlife. It also offers oddness. Numerous stories of UFO sightings and supposed cattle mutilations have occurred in this region where mountain lions are known to prowl.

Still, when in the Rocky Mountains, the thing you must be most careful of is Man.

While here, visit **Montana**, where the elevation of the nearby mountains is higher than most of their town's populations and the only vegetarians are people who suck at hunting.

Then perhaps you can pop over to **Idaho**, where you can see thousands of potatoes as well as white supremacists. Drive over the border to Washington to get weed—and a blowjob if there's time.

Don't forget **Utah**, the land of religious oddness and families with a million children. How do you keep a Mormon from drinking all your beer if you invite him over? Invite two Mormons.

Then there is **Wyoming**; it isn't the end of the world but you can see it from there. In Wyoming, there are two seasons: winter and construction.

Lastly, there's **Colorado**, where everyone is super nice, totally gorgeous, and all holding the best weed. Somehow, you'll hate them anyway.

MISSOULA, MONTANA

Wayne Nance—aka the
Missoula Mauler
Kills: 6+
Span of Activity: April 1974 to
September 1986

Fun Fact: Nance bragged about wanting to kill people as a teenager

From North Dakota, let's head west to Missoula, Montana. Missoula is a town on the move—well, sort of—known for its natural beauty and outdoor activities. If you're in Missoula, make sure you check out the Rattlesnake National Recreation Area & Wilderness, where you can vibe on scenic lakes, wildlife, and enjoy miles of trails for hiking, biking, and cross-country skiing. Missoula is famous for its trout fishing, made famous by the movie (based on the book) *A River Runs Through It.* When you're done busting it outside all day, you can relax in one of Missoula's restaurants or breweries, where you can see lots of people dressed like Woody from *Toy Story.*

You can also check out Greenough Park, where they used to keep bears in cages. Imagine the joy of being so close to historical animal cruelty.

Wayne Nance was born on October 18, 1955, in Clinton, Montana. When Nance was a teenager, he spent much time worshipping the Devil and even branded Satanic symbols on himself with a hot coat hanger. Most people who do such things are branded as posers. Sadly, Nance was not a poser.

In 1974, Donna Pounds came home to find Nance in her bedroom, which must have been seriously awful. He raped her, then shot her in the back of the head with her husband's gun. He was never charged with her murder.

Shortly afterwards, Nance joined the Navy. He lasted a few years but was eventually discharged after he was found in possession of LSD, weed, and a bunch of stolen items.

After his discharge, Nance spent some time in Seattle, Washington. Shortly after he arrived, fifteen-year-old runaway Devonna Nelson went missing. She was found a few weeks later in Missoula, discarded like a piece of trash against a chain-link fence. Later, the body of Marci Bachmann, sixteen, was found, buried in a grave so shallow her leg was still sticking out of it. What's the point of burying a body at all if you're going to leave the leg sticking out? I'm not the most observant person, but come on. Marci was last seen with Nance.

But Nance wasn't done. The body of Janet Lee Lucas was spotted just a few miles away from the final resting place of Bachmann. She had been shot in the head.

Nance was employed delivering furniture around the same time as his murders. One afternoon, he delivered a couch to the home of Michael and Teresa Shook. They were found stabbed to death in their home a few days later.

On September 3, 1986, Nance was found hanging out in the bushes outside the home of his boss, Doug Wells. This probably goes without saying, but it's never a good thing when you come home and find one of your employees lurking in the bushes outside of your house. Wells asked Nance what da fuq he was doing there. Nance said he just happened to be driving by when he saw someone lurking next to the house and was now looking for him.

Yeah. *Riiiight.* "What are you doing lurking in the bushes?"

"Oh, just looking for someone I saw lurking in the bushes!"

Nance somehow recovered from this ridiculous excuse and talked his way inside, assaulted Doug, and then tied him and his wife, Kris, up. He stabbed Doug and left him for dead. But Doug was able to free himself and shot Nance to death as he attempted to rape Kris.

Nance had numerous photos of Kris in his wallet that he had taken of her surreptitiously while she was out jogging. A photo album was found in his home filled with photos of Kris and notes that said things like, "I love you" and "I want you to live with me." Nance was one of those rare killers who managed to be awful and pathetic at the same time.

While you're in the area, check out the Garnet Ghost Town, a historic mining town that offers a wonderful ghost town experience. There was a time, a hundred years ago, that Garnet was a thriving town, filled with gold miners and their families, working hard to carve out a community in the heart of the Garnet Mountains. In 1898, somewhere around a thousand people called Garnet their home. Now, they're all dead. So check it out.

WYOMING

Keith Jesperson—aka the Happy
Face Killer
Kills: 8+
Span of Activity: January 1990 to
March 1995

Fun Fact: Jesperson's childhood nickname was Igor

From Missoula, let's head south to Cheyenne, Wyoming, a city filled with rich Western history that no one cares about. The biggest deal in town is the Cheyenne Frontier Days Rodeo; the long wait times are a drag but being able to witness animals suffering more than makes up for it. After the rodeo, most locals stave off the boredom by getting drunk or smoking meth, depending on their social strata.

Keith Jesperson was born on April 6, 1955. His father was an abusive drunk, and Jesperson was teased both at home and at school. Jesperson also stated he was raped at fourteen. Jesperson decided he didn't GAF about much early in life. He attempted to kill two different boys before he was fifteen.

When Jesperson was twenty, he married, and they had three children. His marriage lasted fourteen years and he worked as a truck driver. While on the road, his wife took the kids and left him. Ironically, she left Jesperson because he was having affairs, not because of violent behavior, but she must have sensed the impending storm.

Jesperson's first victim was Taunja Bennett, whom he met near Portland, Oregon, at a bar in January 1990. He brought her home, strangled her to death, and disposed of her body.

In August 1992, a Jane Doe identified only as "Claudia" was raped and killed. Her body was found near Blythe, California. Her identity remains unknown. A month later, in Turlock,

California, the body of Cynthia Lyn Rose was discovered. Jesperson claimed Rose was a sex worker. His next victim was another sex worker, Laurie Pentland of Salem, Oregon, whose body was found in November 1992.

After he killed Bennett, Jesperson wrote a confession on the bathroom wall of a truck stop and signed it with a smiley face. He later sent other letters to the media and police, which he signed with a smiley face as well, thus earning him the moniker "The Happy Face Killer." One has to give him some credit for having such a good attitude about the whole thing. Life is what you make of it, after all.

According to Jesperson, in January 1995, he picked up Angela Subrize in Spokane, Washington, and told her he'd give her a ride to Fort Collins, Colorado. That didn't happen. He killed her in Cheyenne, bound her body with rope, and dragged her body behind his truck for miles. Then he untied her mangled body and threw it into a ditch.

Jesperson was arrested on March 30, 1995, for the murder of Julie Winningham. Winningham apparently had been his girlfriend for a time. Friends who knew she was dating a tall trucker named Keith eventually led investigators to the six-foot-six Jesperson.

Jesperson claimed to have had as many as 160 victims, but only eight women have been confirmed. He is serving three consecutive life sentences at the Oregon State Penitentiary in Salem, presumably smiling a lot.

On your way out of Cheyenne, check out the Terry Bison Ranch Resort, where you can get right up close to the damn bison. While there, try a Dirty Dan Magee Burger or try events like Dance in the Buff.

The mind reels.

COLORADO

John Agrue
Kills: 3
Span of Activity: July 21, 1966, and June to July 1982

Head south a little bit from Cheyenne and you'll get to Boulder, a perfect balance of urban life and the outdoors. That is, if you're rich. If not, there's a bridge nearby you can sleep under. The city is just thirty miles northwest of Denver, where the Rocky Mountains meet the Plains. Boulder is one of the hippest places anywhere, which means techies, gentrification, and twenty-three-dollar cheeseburgers. Boulder may have once been cool, but the counterculture oddballs have been forced out, leaving Boulder to a bunch of rich old assbags.

Speaking of assbags, on July 21, 1966, an eighteen-year-old Agrue was hanging out with his fifteen-year-old sister-in-law when he started making moves on her. She was like, "Umm, no," so he did what any married eighteen-year-old who was trying to cheat on his wife with his underage sister-in-law would do: he stabbed her a dozen times, killing her. Agrue later told his wife he killed her sister, but she didn't believe him. This lack of awareness isn't surprising since she married an eighteen-year-old psycho. He was arrested two days later and sentenced to twenty-to-fifty years.

He was paroled in 1982, but sadly, he was still weird. A few months after being let out, he stabbed to death twenty-year-old Susan Beckers and dumped her body in the Boulder Canyon. A week later, Agrue stabbed to death his neighbor, ninety-four-year-old Orma Smith, and dumped her body in

the Big Elk Creek Meadows, where it was found the following day.

Agrue was out of his mind. Six days after that, he attempted to abduct a woman at knifepoint on the University of Colorado—Boulder campus but was thankfully busted at the scene.

Agrue was convicted of the attempted abduction and sentenced to prison, but was paroled again in 1989.

It appears that he kept his nose clean from then on. On June 29, 2009, Agrue overdosed on prescription pills at his home. Women's purses were found in his home as well as articles about the murders of Becker and Smith. Later, his DNA was matched to the Smith crime scene.

It's odd how some of these dudes just stop. Some of these dudes simply age out, their urges lessening as their self-control increases.

Before you leave Boulder, check out the Boulder County Farmers Market, one of the most highly regarded farmers markets in Colorado, with a thriving online marketplace and food access programs providing healthy food for hundreds of families in Boulder County. If you don't need fresh produce, jams, and bread, buy your mom some flowers.

DENVER, COLORADO

Vincent Groves
Kills: 7-20
Span of Activity: June 1978 to July 1988

Just half an hour south of Boulder is Denver, with many cool things to do, including museums, historic districts, outdoor activities, and sports. Check out LoDo, which stands for Lower Downtown, a historic area with Victorian buildings that now house restaurants, galleries, and shops. People in Denver clearly don't have time to pronounce entire words.

While in Denver, go kayaking on the Platte River or simply go to a craft brewery and talk to other pretentious hippies with trust funds about how the altitude doesn't bother you.

Vincent Groves was born on April 19, 1954. His family lived in an upper-middle-class suburb of Denver, and his parents were (in theory) nice as all get out. Groves was the only Black student in his high school class. He played basketball for Coe College in Cedar Rapids, Iowa, but he soon dropped out and got a job as an electrician.

In late 1977, Groves branched out from electrical work and became the pimp for seventeen-year-old Jeanette Baca. Before long, she went missing, her naked body found in the woods in June 1978. A few months later, Groves moved in with twenty-one-year-old Norma Jean Halford. She went missing shortly afterwards as well. Her body hasn't been located to this day.

Groves then met and married a woman named Janet Hill, who apparently either didn't care or wasn't aware of Groves'

proclivities. He had always been into drugs, but around this time, he really started using heavily.

Hill convinced Groves to turn himself in when he killed seventeen-year-old Tammy Sue Woodrum while out camping. Come on, who would go camping with Vincent Groves? He claimed Woodrum died from an overdose, which explains everything. Apparently, in Groves' world, "camping" meant doing drugs outside. I wish my parents knew this growing up; it certainly would have improved some family vacations.

He was convicted and sentenced to prison but released on mandatory parole just a few years later. Hill was long gone at this point so he moved in with his parents.

In March 1987, he attempted to strangle a twenty-year-old sex worker in a motel room, but he was so damn loud, witnesses intervened and Groves fled.

Vincent Groves was arrested and questioned about the attack in the motel room. While in custody, DNA linked him to the murders of nineteen-year-old Juanita Lovato and twenty-five-year-old Diane Mancera. He was a suspect in the murders of at least twenty women from Denver who'd been strangled to death.

Groves was convicted of Lovato's killing, receiving life imprisonment. He died on October 31, 1996, in a prison hospital near Denver.

The 12 Volt Tavern is a must to hit before you leave Denver. This biker bar's interior still looks like it hasn't seen the light of day in decades. Get a pickle shot, play some pool, darts, or *Big Buck Hunter* while you listen to classic rock at full blast.

TRINIDAD, COLORADO

Judy Buenoano
Kills: 3
Span of Activity: September 1971
to June 1983

Fun Fact: Buenoano was the first woman to be executed in Florida since 1848

Three hours south of Denver is Trinidad, Colorado, a historic town with a thriving arts scene, museums, and outdoor activities. Trinidad was a stop on the Santa Fe Trail and home to trappers, traders, and ranchers. It was also home to gangster Al Capone for a while. Trinidad is known for protecting the rights of coal miners back in the day, and more currently was known as the "sex change capital of the world" due to the large number of transgender people seeking surgery there.

So if you're a transgender mine worker, have I got a house for you.

Buenoano was born in Quanah, Texas, on April 4, 1943. Her mother died when she was four, and her father remarried. She was reportedly abused by her father and stepmother; they starved her and forced her to work as a slave. She obviously wasn't down with such treatment. When she was fourteen, she spent two months in prison for attacking her father, stepmother, and two stepbrothers with hot grease.

This was the first, but not the last, sign that Judy don't play. She was released and went to reform school, which obviously didn't do a damn thing for her.

Later, she became a nurse's assistant, and had a son named Michael, whom she resented throughout his life due to him being born out of wedlock.

She first married James Goodyear, a sergeant in the United States Air Force. He died on September 16, 1971, in Orlando, Florida. His death was believed to be due to natural causes.

It wasn't.

Two years later, she moved to Trinidad, Colorado, moving in with Bobby Joe Morris. Shockingly, he also died by what were thought to be natural causes.

In 1979, Buenoano's son Michael was diagnosed with paraplegia. In 1980, they went out canoeing one day in Florida, and he drowned. Another horrible accident! Oh my.

In 1983, Buenoano was in a relationship with John Gentry, whom we can all acknowledge had very bad taste in women. His car exploded, injuring him severely. Police found that the "vitamin pills" that Buenoano had been giving Gentry contained arsenic and paraformaldehyde. Exhumations of Michael Goodyear, James Goodyear, and Bobby Joe Morris showed that all had been given arsenic. Buenoano received substantial life insurance payouts after each death, yet somehow no one ever connected the dots.

In 1984, Buenoano was convicted of the murder of her son Michael and the attempted murder of Gentry. She received a twelve-year sentence for the attempted murder charge and a life sentence for the Michael Buenoano murder. In 1985, she was convicted of the murder of her first husband, James Goodyear, and was sentenced to death.

She was incarcerated at the Florida Department of Corrections' Broward Correctional Institution's Death Row for women. On March 30, 1998, Buenoano was executed in the electric chair at the Florida State Prison. When asked if she had any last words, she said, "No, sir." Buenoano's body was cremated. She was the first woman to be executed in

Florida since 1848 and the first woman in the United States to be electrocuted since 1976.

Trinidad's Let the Good Times Roll is the oldest running rink in Colorado. It was established in 1942 to provide the community with a positive distraction in the shadow of WWII. Over the years, it has provided a safe place for kids and families to escape the world and enjoy a few hours of simple joy. The kind of joy one doesn't get while being drowned or poisoned.

THOMPSON SPRINGS, UTAH

Phillip Jablonski
Kills: 5
Span of Activity: July 1978 to April 1991

Named for E.W. Thompson, who lived near the springs and operated a sawmill to the north near the Book Cliffs, is Thompson Springs. It's basically a ghost town now, but not the type anyone would care to see. There's still an exit from I-70 into the town but its old businesses are all closed. The only good thing about no one living in Thompson Springs anymore is if you show up there, you won't have to deal with many polygamists. At last check, ninety-nine residents lived in the town. It's unclear if that's all one family.

Like many of these psychotic freakshows, Jablonksi had a difficult childhood; his father was an alcoholic who was violent towards his wife and children.

Jablonski met his first wife, Alice McGowan, in high school. The relationship wasn't all that romantic as he often strangled her until she passed out. Apparently, McGowan eventually became concerned about this and left him.

Jablonski became involved with Jane Sanders in 1968. He raped Sanders on their first date, which apparently wasn't enough to make her think twice about hanging out with him, or to report him. After many years of abuse, including him pulling a gun on her when she wanted to stop having sex, she left him in 1972.

In February 1977, Jablonski met Linda Kimball in Palm Springs. By August, they were living together. On July 6,

1978, Kimball's mother woke up to Jablonksi standing next to her bed. He told her he was going to rape her, but he couldn't go through with it as every time he looked at her "all he could see was Linda's face." What a smooth talker.

A few days later, Kimball left Jablonski. Why did it take her days? If there's one thing for sure, Jablonski had some sort of pipeline to women with low self-esteem. She returned on July 16, 1978, to pick up belongings for their baby. She was found dead in the apartment that afternoon. She'd been beaten, stabbed, and strangled. Jablonski was arrested eleven days later and served twelve years in prison for Kimball's murder before he was released for good behavior.

Soon after, he married Carol Spadoni, whom he'd started communicating with while still in prison. In 1991, he murdered Spadoni and her mother, whom he also sexually assaulted for good measure.

He then killed Fathyma Vann in Indio, California. He shot her in the head, sexually assaulted her, and carved "I ♥ Jesus" in her back.

Jablonski was finally taken off the streets after the murder of Margie Rogers, fifty-eight, in Grand County, Utah. She was a classmate of Jablonski at a community college. She was shot in the head and sexually assaulted. He was found guilty of her murder and sentenced to death.

Jablonski died on December 27, 2019, of "unknown causes" at the age of seventy-three in San Quentin State Prison in his cell.

Sego Canyon, Utah, is just west of the Colorado border along US Route 70, a few miles away from Thompson Springs. Indigenous people painted and carved images on the canyon walls. Those ghostly forms are still on display today, provocative, mysterious, and enduring reminders of the people who lived here long ago.

SALT LAKE CITY, UTAH

Roberto Arguelles—aka the Salt Lake City Strangler
Kills: 4+
Span of Activity: February to March 1982

A bit northwest of Thompson City is Salt Lake City, a modern city with a variety of attractions, including outdoor activities, parks, and cultural venues, and whose slogan is "Salt Lake City is Cooler Than You Think." Sadly, it isn't, unless to you "cool" equals Mormons, wildfires, bad air quality, and small pours.

Roberto V. Arguelles was born on February 14, 1962, in Kearns, Utah. In 1978, he was arrested for kidnapping and molesting a ten-year-old girl, and, in a separate case, of raping a seventeen-year-old. He was found guilty of both charges and placed in the Youth Development Center in Oden until he was twenty-one years old.

This did absolutely nothing for him.

When he got out, he kidnapped a fifteen-year-old girl and raped her. Three days later, he picked up a fourteen-year-old girl and drove her to a dirt road where he raped her as well. She fought like a mofo so Arguelles slashed her throat and dumped her in the street, leaving her for dead.

She wasn't though.

She was able to get help after walking to a nearby house and getting treated at the local hospital. She gave a description of Arguelles and his truck, leading to Arguelles' arrest. He pleaded guilty to two counts of attempted murder, aggravated rape, and sexual abuse. Arguelles was paroled on June 25, 1991.

His stint in prison also did absolutely nothing for him.

On August 1, 1992, posing as a security guard at the local elementary school, Arguelles approached a brother and a sister, eight and ten years old respectively. Under the pretense of frisking them to look for stolen goods, he pulled down their pants, touching the boy's genitals and patting the girl's crotch. He then dropped them off at home.

Because that's what security guards do.

A week later, he used a fake police badge in an attempt to trick two ten-year-old girls into getting in his car. However, he was spotted by a witness, who notified the police.

Arguelles was arrested and charged with molesting the siblings from Orchard Elementary School; because of his priors, he was found guilty and sentenced to life imprisonment with the possibility of parole.

Three years later, while in prison, Arguelles began running his mouth and talking, occasionally bragging to cellmates about killing a few young girls and women in 1992, and making ransom demands from their families. Always a bright idea, right? Eventually, this attracted the attention of investigators. When interviewed for the first time in July 1995, he confessed to the murders of sixteen-year-old Lisa Martinez and fifteen-year-old Tuesday Roberts; both girls vanished while walking towards the Valley Fair Mall on March 30, 1992. Arguelles said he stabbed Martinez at least forty-three times with a wood chisel, before strangling Roberts with a rope. Authorities discovered the girls' gravesites near Arguelles' stepfather's pig farm after he directed authorities in that direction.

Several months later, he confessed to two additional murders: forty-two-year-old high school janitor Margo Bond, and thirteen-year-old Stephanie Blundell. Both were found stabbed to death, Bond in Tooele County and Blundell in

American Fork Canyon. Following her murder, Arguelles showed some of Blundell's jewelry to Pamela Milstein, a prison inmate who corroborated the claims from when she lived with him and his mother.

Arguelles was later charged in all four deaths. On June 21, 1997, Arguelles was sentenced to death with his chosen method being the firing squad. He began to exhibit messed-up behavior in prison, including eating his own feces. He died in his cell in 2003 because of "bowel obstruction."

I don't even want to know.

The Salt Lake Whale, officially titled *Out of the Blue*, is a sculpture located at a roundabout in the Ninth and Ninth neighborhood of Salt Lake City. It was universally hated at first, so much so that now it's become ridiculously cool.

All hail the whale.

OGDEN, UTAH

Ray Gardner
Kills: 3
Span of Activity: 1941 to August 1949

Just a bit north of Salt Lake City is Ogden. There are many cool things to do in Ogden, Utah, including museums, parks, historic sites, and other attractions, like the Ogden Dinosaur Park.

Ogden is known as a rough town. Its reputation in Utah is as "Sin City." Which is kind of like being the tallest dwarf.

Ray Gardner was raised in an orphanage in Columbus, Ohio. He spent his entire life on the wrong side of the law, committing over five hundred crimes, and spending time at the Indiana Boys School, the Montana State Prison, and the Wyoming State Penitentiary.

In 1941, Gardner strangled his cellmate, Frank Shelley, in a jail in North Dakota. It was thought at the time that Shelley died of natural causes. Although it seems to me that "it was thought at the time" means no one cared.

On July 20, 1949, in Ogden, Utah, Gardner picked up seventeen-year-old Shirley Gretzinger, who thought she was on her way to a babysitting job. He stuffed paper down her throat and raped her as she was dying. Gardner left her body lying in a thicket.

Gardner then went to Montana, where he met thirty-nine-year-old Sue Horn. When Gardner tried to take her money, Horn refused and slapped him. Gardner then shot her, took

her belongings, and buried her. Slapping a serial killer doesn't work often.

In August 1949, Gardner drove through a stop sign and hit an overturned trailer. The police became suspicious after they found Horn's luggage and clothing in the car and realized she was missing. These guys were obviously deep thinkers. He confessed to killing Horn, and to killing Gretzinger and Shelley.

He was found guilty of first-degree murder. Gardner was executed by firing squad at the Utah State Prison on September 29, 1951. Gardner's last words were, "I'm ready to go. No one will miss me. My life has been worthless."

Before getting out of Ogden, check out Peery's Egyptian Theater. A historic, architectural jewel in the heart of Ogden and built in an era of sumptuous movie palaces, this 1924 theater, designed to replicate the courtyard between two Egyptian temples, has been returned to its original elegance. This all leads people in Ogden to ask the old question: *Where am I? Utah or Egypt?*

JOHNNY TREVISANI with BRIAN WHITNEY

IDAHO FALLS, IDAHO

Paul Rhoades
Kills: 3-7
Span of Activity: February to
March 1987

A few hours north of Ogden is Idaho Falls, Idaho, with many cool attractions, including parks, museums, and outdoor areas, including Snake River.

Idaho likes its guns. Well over half the people in Idaho own guns. The state is known for having some of the most lenient gun laws in the nation. While there, you can use your gun to shoot rattlesnakes, scorpions, bats, black widows, and brown recluse spiders. Because that shit is everywhere.

Speaking of guns, Paul Ezra Rhoades was born on January 18, 1957, in Idaho Falls. Rhoades had polio since the age of four, and for which he constantly had to be hospitalized.

At the age of ten, he began drinking heavily, at least heavily for a ten-year-old, and dropped out of school. At around the same time, he started using various drugs, but meth was his favorite. Like most enterprising meth heads, he started breaking into homes, stealing any valuables he could find.

On the morning of March 1, 1987, the body of twenty-one-year-old Stacy Dawn Baldwin, a store clerk who was working the night shift, was found. She had been shot three times. Soon after, on March 17, twenty-year-old Nolan Haddon, a clerk working at a convenience store in Idaho Falls, was found murdered in the store's walk-in cooler.

Four days later, the body of thirty-four-year-old Susan Michelbacher was found in a field. Rhoades had abducted her from the parking lot of a supermarket and forced her to cash two $1,000 checks at a bank. She was shot nine times and then raped, quite possibly after she was already dead.

On March 27, 1987, Rhoades was arrested on a warrant in Wells, Nevada. His handgun's bullets were a match to the ones used in the recent murders. Rhoades was charged with Michelbacher's murder, He was found guilty and sentenced to death. After the sentence was read out, he grabbed the chair he had been sitting in and threw it at the prosecutor. This appears to be one of those "don't shoot the messenger" vibes.

He was executed via lethal injection on November 18, 2011. As his final statement, Rhoades addressed his mother and executioners, stating he forgave them, before confessing that he indeed had committed the Michelbacher killing, and apologizing to her husband. Rhodes is a suspect in at least four more murders.

If you're in Idaho Falls, check out D'railed, a unique restaurant located in an old converted house next to the railway tracks. They say the "small establishment exudes a bohemian, punk vibe with eclectic decor and interesting clientele."

You can be the judge of that.

THE FAR WEST

The Far West region of the United States is less a unified territory and more a bizarre family reunion where no one really gets along but they all still show up for the photo. It contains six states—Alaska, Washington, Oregon, California, Nevada, and Hawaii—each with its own distinct personality disorder; yet somehow, they all fall under the same regional umbrella.

Alaska is the cranky uncle who moved off grid to avoid "the government" but still manages to collect Social Security. It's stunningly beautiful, dangerously cold, and home to the kind of people use "bear repellent" as cologne.

Washington is the tech-savvy older sibling who drinks too much coffee, wears expensive hiking gear to the grocery store, and has very strong opinions about sustainable farming despite never having touched dirt. It's also where billionaires go to build spaceships, because apparently Earth isn't doing it for them anymore.

Oregon is Washington's weirder, thriftier, hipster cousin who insists everything was better before anyone else discovered it. Portland is what happens when you smoke too much weed and create a city based on craft beer, artisanal doughnuts, and a deeply concerning number of adults who own pet goats. The rest of the state is either a lush green wonderland or a barren high desert, depending on which direction you accidentally get lost in.

California is the overachieving sibling who simultaneously wins every award and still makes the worst life choices. It has Silicon Valley billionaires, Hollywood dreamers, and a growing population of people who've been priced out of their own homes but refuse to leave because, let's be honest, the weather is unbeatable. Every year, half the state is on fire and the other half is sitting in traffic trying to get to brunch.

Nevada is that sketchy cousin who somehow always has cash but no visible source of income. The entire state is essentially a neon mirage built on slot machines, desert, and poor decision making. People come here to "let loose" and leave with fewer teeth and more regrets, and honestly, that's exactly the business model.

Hawaii is the distant relative who only shows up for special occasions and makes everyone jealous. It's absurdly beautiful, mostly chill, and quietly resents the way tourists treat it like their personal playground. The locals have mastered the art of side-eyeing while selling you a twelve-dollar piña colada.

Together, these states make up the Far West—an area that's equal parts stunning, strange, and slightly unhinged. Whether you're dodging bears, debating which organic milk alternative is superior, or losing your life savings on a craps table, this region has something for everyone. Just don't ask them to agree on anything.

Happy trails, travel in pairs, and maybe don't take that shortcut through the woods.

ANCHORAGE, ALASKA

Robert Hansen—aka the Butcher Baker
Kills: 17+
Span of Activity: December 1971 to April 1983

Start your tour in Anchorage, Alaska's largest city and home to Robert Hansen, the Butcher Baker. Hansen ran a bakery by day and hunted women for sport by night, which gives a whole new meaning to bakers who make bear claws. Hansen eventually admitted to murdering a total of seventeen women, but who knows if making bear claws all day gave him ideas.

Anchorage is the kind of place where people move to get away from it all, only to realize that "it all" includes basic amenities like sunlight and vegetables that aren't frozen. It's the largest city in Alaska, which is a little like being the tallest person at a hobbit convention—technically impressive, but still a niche achievement.

For half the year, Anchorage is a frozen tundra where residents pretend that scraping ice off their windshields at three a.m. builds character. The other half, it's an all-you-can-eat mosquito buffet with twenty-two hours of daylight, ensuring that no one ever really sleeps or stops questioning their life choices. The city itself is a mix of rugged wilderness and suburban sprawl, where you can buy a Frappuccino, spot a moose at the drive-thru, and still get chased by a bear before lunch.

The locals pride themselves on their ability to function in subzero temperatures, making them insufferable to anyone considering "light sweater weather" a crisis. They're also deeply committed to their belief that Anchorage is "not like

the rest of Alaska," which is a bold claim for a place where you can still lose your dog to an eagle.

Culturally, Anchorage is an eclectic mix of people who either love adventure or are actively avoiding the IRS. It has a thriving arts scene, if you count taxidermy as an art form, and a downtown that looks like it was designed by someone who once saw a city in a magazine but wasn't totally convinced by the concept.

Anchorage is weird, beautiful, a little dangerous, and constantly covered in either snow or salmon. It's the kind of place where the line between "thriving" and "just surviving" is very, very thin—but that's exactly how the locals like it. But even for Anchorage, Robert Hansen was weird.

Robert Hansen was what happens when a socially awkward baker with serious mommy issues decides that hunting actual people sounds like a fun extracurricular. Born in 1939, he spent his early years under the eye of an authoritative father who forced his son into the pastry business. Later, while in high school, he was bullied for his acne, his stutter, and, presumably, just generally creeping people out. Instead of developing a normal hobby—like, say, fishing or aggressively over seasoning food—Hansen took up arson and developed a deep, unsettling hatred for women. Always a great combo.

By the 1970s and '80s, Hansen had settled in Alaska, where he ran a bakery and built up a solid reputation as the town's friendly, unassuming guy—if you ignored the part where he was secretly kidnapping, assaulting, and murdering women. His method? Kidnapping sex workers and dancers, flying them in his private plane out to the remote wilderness, and then literally hunting them down for sport. He was known to bring his victims back to his house in Muldoon, a neighborhood of Anchorage.

Despite being arrested multiple times for, you know, violent crimes, police in Anchorage kept letting him off with slaps on the wrist—because why take a guy with a basement full of guns and a list of missing women too seriously? Eventually, an escaped victim led to his capture in 1983, and, surprise surprise, his house was full of souvenirs from his victims, including a literal map marking the locations of his kills. Because if you're going to be a monster, at least be organized.

Hansen was sentenced to life in prison, where he remained until he died in 2014, proving that even the most patient and methodical serial killers eventually run out of time—and places to hide their very incriminating maps.

While you're in town, treat yourself to some salmon. It's best to eat it now because, trust me, you don't want to associate it with Hansen's outdoor "adventures."

Alaska is the perfect destination for adventurers, nature lovers, and those with a morbid fascination for the dark underbelly of humanity. Just remember, while the landscapes are vast and breathtaking, so is the list of ways to get into trouble. Whether you're hiking through remote wilderness or enjoying Anchorage's downtown charm, keep your wits about you. And maybe pack an extra flashlight. After all, in Alaska, you never know what—or who—might be lurking in the shadows. *Bon voyage!*

SEATTLE, WASHINGTON

Ted Bundy
Kills: 20 confirmed, 30 confessed, 36+ suspected
Span of Activity: January 1974 to February 1978

Let's move a little south to the continental part of the country: Seattle, Washington, the city that insists it's cooler than you but doesn't want to make a big deal about it. Nestled between a postcard-perfect mountain range and a body of water that's somehow always too cold to swim in, Seattle is where tech bros, coffee snobs, and Patagonia-clad outdoorsy types coexist in an ecosystem fueled by overpriced lattes and seasonal affective disorder.

Rain? Oh, they don't call it rain—it's a "light mist," which feels like someone's spitting on you in slow motion. Don't worry, though; you'll be handed a cup of artisanal, single-origin coffee at every corner to warm your soggy soul. And if that's not your thing, there's kombucha on tap. Everywhere. It's like the official beverage of hipster optimism.

Washington's history of hosting serial killers—because apparently, that's a thing you can host—has become as much a part of its identity as salmon and bold politeness. The Pacific Northwest seems to have provided a fertile breeding ground for the likes of Ted Bundy, Gary Ridgway (aka the Green River Killer), and a disturbing handful of others who, for reasons we probably shouldn't think too deeply about, felt the rain and gloom were the perfect backdrop for their hobbies.

Still, the state's natural beauty remains unparalleled. Towering mountains, sparkling lakes, and endless forests offer a picturesque distraction from any unsettling thoughts about what might be lurking in the woods.

Born in 1946 at the Elizabeth Lund Home for Unwed Mothers in Burlington, Vermont, Ted Bundy entered the world as Theodore Robert Cowell—because starting off with an alias is a good move when your life will be a train wreck. Raised in a normal family dynamic where his grandparents pretended to be his parents, with his mother playing the role of "that mysterious older sister," Bundy developed a knack for confusing relationships, which he'd later put to horrible use.

As a teenager, Bundy dabbled in hobbies like shoplifting and peeping through windows because, apparently, every future psychopath has to start with an internship. He was the type of guy who could simultaneously charm your grandmother at Thanksgiving and steal your wallet before dessert—sort of like a con artist but with even worse intentions.

Bundy eventually made his way to college in Washington, where he studied psychology. Who better to understand the human mind than someone Hellbent on manipulating it? He later went to law school in Utah (insert lawyers-are-sociopaths joke here).

Despite his smooth-talking demeanor, he wasn't much of a catch in his younger years—more the guy who'd hang out at the corner of the party sipping flat beer and trying to sell you on pyramid schemes. But after getting dumped by his girlfriend in college, Bundy decided to reinvent himself, trading awkwardness for charisma and repressed rage for... well, unrepressed rage.

By around 1974, Ted Bundy had gone from "that weird guy who collects newspaper clippings" to something far more sinister. In January, in the Seattle area, the first of his many victims disappeared, officially kicking off a killing career that would make him infamous and leave the rest of us deeply paranoid about ever accepting help from a handsome stranger with a cast.

While in Seattle, the Space Needle stands as a constant reminder that Seattle once hosted a World's Fair and has been humble-bragging about it ever since. Down below, Pike Place Market offers the chance to buy fish that's been thrown around for sport because why not turn seafood into  performance art? And let's not forget the tech industry, which has singlehandedly made it impossible to buy a home unless you're an Amazon VP or a TikTok influencer who just *really* loves raincoats.

GREEN RIVER, WASHINGTON

Gary Ridgway—aka the Green River Killer
Kills: 49
Span of Activity: July 1982 to January 1998

Fun Fact: Gary had pressured his wife to have sex in public and inappropriate places, "coincidentally" where his victims' bodies were later discovered

Green River Valley is a picture-perfect place. Rolling hills, quaint little towns... the kind of place where you'd expect to find Norman Rockwell painting a wholesome scene of children playing hopscotch.

But oh, the secrets this idyllic valley holds! Beneath those picturesque meadows, nestled amongst the wildflowers, lie the remains of... well, let's just say the local flora has a particular fondness for human fertilizer.

The Green River Valley has a bit of a... reputation. A reputation for... disappearing acts. Folks would vanish without a trace, like mist evaporating on a summer morning. Their loved ones, naturally, would be beside themselves with worry. "Oh dear," they'd fret, "I wonder if dear Aunt Mildred has finally taken up skydiving."

The authorities, bless their souls, would scratch their heads. "Most perplexing," they'd declare. "Truly a baffling mystery!" Little did they suspect that the answer lay not in the heavens, but a few feet beneath their very noses.

Gary Ridgway, better known as the Green River Killer, is proof that sometimes the most terrifying people are also the most aggressively dull. If serial killers had a union, Ridgway would be the guy who always showed up early to meetings, brought his own lunch in a neatly labeled Tupperware, and never quite grasped the concept of "charisma." He was, in short, the human

equivalent of a beige carpet square—deeply unremarkable yet somehow responsible for an alarming number of murders.

During his formative years, Ridgway wet his bed until he was thirteen. His controlling mother would forcefully wash his genitals after every episode. Ridgway would later tell defense psychologists that during that time, he had weird feelings of anger and sexual attraction toward his mother and fantasized about killing her.

Ridgway was also dyslexic, which resulted in being held back a year in high school. I guess his dyslexia wasn't an issue when, at sixteen, he led a six-year-old boy into the woods and stabbed him through the ribs, hitting the boy's liver.

Operating in the Pacific Northwest during the 1980s and 1990s, Ridgway managed to become one of the most prolific serial killers in US history, which is impressive in the same way that eating fifty hot dogs in one sitting is impressive: you don't want to applaud it, but you do have to acknowledge the sheer commitment. He targeted vulnerable women, particularly sex workers, because—like all truly uninspired men—he preferred victims who were unlikely to fight back or be immediately missed.

When he was finally caught in 2001, thanks to DNA evidence and the long arm of science finally getting its act together, everyone was shocked at just how unremarkable he looked. No brooding intensity, no sinister twinkle in the eye—simply a middle-aged guy who looked like he spent his weekends pricing out lawnmowers at Home Depot.

Ridgway confessed to killing at least seventy-one women, though it's likely more, which means he was not only an evil psychopath but also a blatant overachiever. He pleaded guilty to avoid the death penalty, which, given his complete lack of personality, was probably a missed opportunity for the world's most anticlimactic execution. Instead, he's spending the rest of his life in prison, where, one assumes, he has become the kind of inmate who meticulously organizes the commissary shelves and corrects peoples' grammar in letters home.

In the grand hierarchy of serial killers, Ridgway will never be considered "cool" (a deeply unsettling concept in itself), but he will always be a reminder that the most dangerous people aren't always the ones twirling their mustaches in dark alleys—they're sometimes plain, boring men with too much time on their hands and absolutely no moral compass.

And there you have it, folks. Gary Ridgway, a man who truly redefined the term "green thumb."

So, next time you're driving through the Green River Valley, admire the scenery, but perhaps keep your windows rolled up. And if you see a particularly vibrant patch of wildflowers, do try to resist the urge to investigate. You never know what might be lurking beneath the surface.

While here, you might want to do some whitewater rafting. Check out Green River Adventures for some whitewater rafting and waterfall rappelling.

Don't drown.

SALEM, OREGON

Jerry Brudos—aka the
Shoe Fetish Slayer
Kills: 4
Span of Activity: January 1968 to
April 1969

Cross into Oregon, where the motto might as well be "Keep Portland Weird... and Keep Your Doors Locked." Portland offers charming food carts, an endless stream of microbreweries, and Powell's City of Books, which is large enough to hide at least three serial killers (hypothetically speaking).

By the faint glow of a Pacific twilight, the heart of Oregon beckons—a land stitched with untamed rivers, ghostly forests, and stories so thick you might lose yourself in the telling. Yet here, in this verdant cradle of the Pacific Northwest, every trail leads somewhere profound: to beauty, to shadow, and sometimes to the edges of the unknowable.

Nestled between the brooding Pacific coastline and the sentinel peaks of the Cascades, Oregon offers a feast for wanderers who dare to embrace both wonder and unease. One moment, you're in the gentle hum of a vineyard near the Willamette Valley, cradling a glass of pinot noir that whispers of sun-soaked afternoons; the next, you're lost among the mist-shrouded Douglas firs, where the past seems to linger just out of reach.

Jerry Brudos—the Norman Bates starter kit, who took shoe fetish to a level even the most forgiving therapist would describe as "deeply concerning"—was born in 1939 to a mother who wanted a girl instead of a boy. The amiable people-pleaser, trying to gain momma's favor, found a rhinestone-laden pair of stilettos and wore them for his momma. She disapproved of Brudos' gender-busting gesture and punished him. That didn't stop him. Brudos spent his formative years collecting women's shoes like some boys collect baseball cards—except instead of trading them, he stole them and fantasized about murder. Classic childhood hijinks!

By the time puberty hit, Brudos had escalated from stealing heels to full-on abducting, torturing, and murdering women. His preferred method of expressing himself? Keeping trophies—which is just a delicate way of saying he hoarded severed feet like some people hoard Beanie Babies. If that wasn't unsettling enough, he also liked to dress up in women's underwear while wearing said stolen shoes, because even serial killers need to have hobbies.

Operating out of his home outside of Salem, Oregon, in the late 1960s, Brudos managed to kill at least four women, all while maintaining the world's most suspicious-looking garage. Each was brutalized in various ways. Two of his victims were found in Long Tom River, one weighed down by a car part and missing her breasts.

And despite being married with kids, his wife somehow never noticed the creepy Polaroids, the growing collection of body parts, or the fact that he spent a truly unsettling amount of time alone in his "workshop." Apparently, red flags were only for countries.

Eventually, the police caught on (you can only steal so many shoes and murder so many people before someone connects the dots), and Brudos was sentenced to life in prison. He died behind bars in 2006. One wonders if his last words were "rhinestone stilettos."

I suppose you can visit Long Tom River but for a less ominous thrill, visit Crater Lake National Park. It's the deepest lake in the United States, created by a volcanic eruption more than seven thousand years ago. Beautiful, serene, and absolutely perfect for imagining what else might be hiding in those crystal-clear depths.

SANTA CRUZ COUNTY, CALIFORNIA

David Carpenter—aka the
Trailside Killer
Kills: 8-10
Span of Activity: August 1979 to
May 1981

Fun Fact: Carpenter had a severe stutter

Santa Cruz County is what happens when a beach town and a Phish concert have a baby, and that baby grows up to major in Environmental Studies while living in a converted van. Tucked along California's central coast, Santa Cruz is both stunningly beautiful and deeply committed to making sure you know how *chill* it is.

The city of Santa Cruz itself is famous for its surf culture, its vintage boardwalk, and its population of people who look like they own a crystal shop but somehow afford its four-grand-a-month rent. The Santa Cruz Beach Boardwalk is like if Coney Island did yoga—there's a roller coaster older than your grandparents, and the seagulls have evolved into ruthless, fry-stealing crime lords. Meanwhile, downtown is packed with vegan cafés, metaphysical bookstores, and a Trader Joe's parking lot that doubles as an MMA training facility.

Santa Cruz was also home to David Carpenter, a guy who was so good at serial killing that authorities suspected he was the infamous Zodiac Killer. But then the investigators spoke to him and realized he wasn't bright enough to make a cipher.

David Carpenter was the kind of guy who could turn a peaceful walk in the woods into a true crime documentary. Born in 1930, Carpenter spent most of his life proving that some people radiate serial killer energy. Awkward, also a bed-wetter, had a stuttering problem, and was about as charming as a wet sock, he had a knack for making women deeply uncomfortable long before he started murdering them.

After a long and distinguished career of being a creep (which included attempted assaults and a prison stint for attacking women in the '60s), Carpenter decided to upgrade to full-blown serial killer status in the late 1970s and early '80s. His preferred hunting ground? The scenic hiking trails of Northern California. Because, apparently, getting lost, getting poison oak, and being forced to pretend you love hiking weren't enough reasons to avoid the woods—now there was also a psychopath lurking behind every redwood.

With the fashion sense of a disappointed substitute teacher and the charisma of a DMV employee on their last nerve, Carpenter managed to kill at least ten people before authorities finally connected the dots. But despite being about as subtle as a bear in a convenience store, it still took years to catch him. Why? Well, this was the golden age of serial killers, when police departments were basically running on vibes and gut feelings. And bad coffee.

Eventually, DNA evidence (and the fact that literally everyone found him suspicious) led to his arrest in 1981. As of today, he's sitting on death row, proving that even the most unlikable, socially inept serial killers eventually run out of places to hide.

While there, venture south to places like Capitola and Aptos, where the kombucha flows like wine and the word "artisanal" is legally required to appear on at least thirty percent of menus. Watsonville, the agricultural heart of the county, produces world-class strawberries and a deep resentment toward the Tesla-driving transplants who think "farm-to-table" means they invented farming.

And, of course, the locals—an eclectic mix of surfers, Deadheads, aging hippies, trust-fund slackers, and tech workers escaping Silicon Valley but still somehow being Silicon Valley. These are people who will absolutely judge you for using plastic straws, even as they light their second joint of the morning.

LOS ANGELES, CALIFORNIA

Richard Ramirez—aka the Night Stalker
Kills: 15+
Span of Activity: April 1984 to August 1985

Los Angeles is a sprawling, sunburnt, Botox-filled nightmare, where everyone is either chasing fame, pretending they're not chasing fame, or writing a screenplay about someone chasing fame. It's a city where the traffic moves at the speed of emotional healing, and the air quality reminds you that you're slowly marinating in exhaust fumes.

Home to Hollywood, the land of broken dreams and casting couches, L.A. is a place where people pay eighteen dollars for avocado toast and call it self-care. The locals? A fascinating mix of Instagram influencers, failed actors moonlighting as baristas, and tech bros who swear they moved here for the "vibe." If you're looking for an authentic cultural experience, don't bother—everything here is curated, filtered, and lit for optimum engagement.

But let's talk about Richard Ramirez.

Richard Ramirez was the kind of guy who looked like he crawled out of a dumpster behind a Hot Topic and just never left. Born in 1960, he spent his formative years dabbling in petty crime, worshiping Satan, and perfecting the aesthetic of a man who hasn't slept, showered, or seen sunlight in at least a decade. If there had been a Craigslist ad for "Satanic Drifter Seeking Like-Minded Chaos," Ramirez would have been the first to respond.

Between 1984 and 1985, Ramirez went on a rampage road trip across California that was so random and brutal, it was as if he was actively trying to make crime statistics unreadable. He used Glassell Park in Los Angeles as his own dumping ground. Breaking into homes at night, he attacked men, women, and children with the enthusiasm of someone playing a particularly unhinged round of *Grand Theft Auto*. He had no set pattern, no clear motive—just a love for breaking and entering, violence, and looking like a rejected member of an '80s goth band.

And yet, despite his complete lack of subtlety (leaving footprints, fingerprints, and his literal shoe size at crime scenes), the police took way too long to catch him. This was the '80s, after all—a time when forensic science was basically just squinting at blurry Polaroids and police departments still thought "serial killer" was a made-up concept.

When Ramirez was finally identified, he fled L.A. like a man who realized his hotel doesn't offer free breakfast. But his master escape plan—running down the street in broad daylight—didn't work out so well. Instead of a dramatic final stand, he was recognized by a group of civilians who proceeded to beat the absolute Hell out of him before the cops showed up.

At trial, Ramirez spent most of his time making dramatic Satanic proclamations, flashing his pentagram-covered palm, and acting like the world's least-likable rock star. Unfortunately for him, neither Satan nor his terrible fashion choices could save him from being sentenced to death. He spent decades in prison before dying in 2013, proving that even the most overconfident, hygiene-averse serial killers eventually run out of time—and hairspray.

After checking out the Night Stalker's playground, L.A. offers something for everyone: the beaches are gorgeous but packed with tourists and sand that sticks to places it shouldn't, the hills are great if you enjoy pretending you like hiking, and downtown is where you go if you want to pay seven dollars for a bottle of water and still step over human feces.

Well, for the most part, L.A.'s weather, always perfect, would be nice if it didn't make you feel like a failure for staying inside. But don't worry, the constant threat of wildfires, earthquakes, and influencers recording TikToks in traffic keeps things  exciting. They don't call it LaLa Land for nothing.

CROSS POLICE LINE DO NOT CROSS POLICE
POLICE LINE DO NOT CROSS POLIC
CROSS POLICE LINE DO NOT CROSS POLI

WASHOE COUNTY, NEVADA

James Richard Curry
Kills: 4-5
Span of Activity: 1982 to 1983

Fun Fact: Curry was employed as a locksmith

Washoe County, Nevada, is what happens when someone starts designing a postcard but gets distracted halfway through. It's a place where the desert meets the high Sierra, where casinos and sagebrush coexist in a tenuous truce, and where the residents have perfected the art of looking both ruggedly independent and vaguely annoyed at the same time.

Reno, the county seat, thinks of itself as Vegas' scrappy younger sibling—the one that got into community college and never left town. Here, cowboy hats are not a fashion statement but a municipal requirement, and slot machines lurk in every gas station like friendly, one-armed bandits just waiting to make you regret that extra gallon of unleaded.

James Richard Curry isn't exactly a household name in the world of serial killers, which is probably for the best. If you're going to be infamous, you should at least have a name with some pizzazz—like the Midnight Strangler or the Nevada Nibbler. But no, James Richard Curry sounds like the guy who fixes your air conditioning and overcharges you for freon.

Curry was the human embodiment of every bad Tinder date you've ever had, except instead of just ghosting people or talking too much about cryptocurrency, he *murdered* them. Born in 1946, Curry's claim to fame was proving that you don't need to be a criminal mastermind to be a full-blown psychopath, just deeply unstable and *really* bad at relationships.

Curry wasn't specifically associated with only Nevada; he killed people in California too. Even serial killers need a change in scenery.

He met one victim in Washoe County, Nevada. And by met, I mean he sexually assaulted and shot her in the back of the head. Her body was later dumped along the Sheep's Flat hiking trail near Incline Village, where it was soon found by hikers.

In the end, James Richard Curry did what most criminals do— he faded into the annals of history, overshadowed by more theatrically unhinged murderers. But for a brief moment in time, he was proof that even the most nondescript people can have the absolute worst hobbies.

If you want something to visit, head to Lake Tahoe, Washoe's crown jewel, where Californians flood in every winter to ski and every summer to complain about the price of lakefront Airbnbs. It's stunningly beautiful in a way that makes you wonder if you should apologize for being there.

The rest of the county is a lawless expanse of open desert, punctuated by the occasional dust devil and a suspiciously enthusiastic "world's largest" something-or-other. And somewhere out there, between the tumbleweeds and the world's loneliest rest stop, a coyote is probably judging your life choices.

HONOLULU, HAWAII

The Honolulu Strangler
Kills: 5
Span of Activity: May 1985 to April 1986

Hop on a plane to Hawaii, one of the most beautiful places on Earth.

Honolulu is the kind of place where people spend thousands of dollars to sit in traffic while wearing a floral shirt they bought at an airport gift shop. Located on the Hawaiian island of Oahu, it's a tropical paradise—if your idea of paradise includes overpriced Mai Tais, confused tourists trying to hula, and locals who have perfected the art of politely resenting you.

The beaches are stunning, the water is crystal clear, and yes, Waikiki looks exactly like a postcard—if that postcard also included sunburned Midwesterners fighting over a beach chair. Meanwhile, downtown Honolulu offers a thrilling mix of high-end designer stores, historic landmarks, and the occasional wild chicken, just to keep things interesting.

Then there's the cost of living, which is so astronomical that even the palm trees are considering getting a second job. Locals work multiple gigs to afford rent, while tourists drop a small fortune on luaus, including exactly one spoonful of poi and a deeply awkward fire dance performance.

The Honolulu Strangler, Hawaii's first (and hopefully last) known serial killer, was active in the mid-1980s, proving that even a place famous for sunshine and Mai Tais isn't immune to true crime. Apparently, someone took one look at the swaying palm trees, the turquoise water, and the general Aloha vibe and thought, *You know what this place needs? Absolute terror.*

Between 1985 and 1986, five women were found murdered, all strangled and dumped in various locations around Oahu. The pattern was obvious—enough so that the police launched Hawaii's first real serial killer investigation. But because this was the '80s, when forensic science was basically just guesswork with a badge, the case was handled with all the precision of a tipsy tourist trying to pronounce "Humuhumunukunukuapua'a."

The prime suspect was a guy who failed a polygraph, had a suspicious history, and whose wife straight-up told police that he was probably the killer. But since "probably" wasn't enough to hold up in court, the investigation hit a dead end. Instead of an arrest, the murders just stopped, leaving the case unsolved to this day—because if there's one thing scarier than a serial killer, it's an unsolved serial killer case.

The Honolulu Strangler: the ultimate reminder that even in paradise, there's always that one guy who ruins it for everyone.

But while you're in paradise, let's not forget Pearl Harbor, where visitors reflect on history in the most American way possible—by buying a commemorative T-shirt.

For More News About Johnny Trevisani and Brian Whitney, Signup For Our Newsletter:

http://wbp.bz/newsletter

Word-of-mouth is critical to an author's long-term success. If you appreciated this book please leave a review on the Amazon sales page:

https://wbp.bz/SerialKillerTravelGuideReviews

ALSO AVAILABLE FROM WILDBLUE PRESS

"*You want to know what happened? Ask Anne.*"
—serial killer William Devin Howell

HIS GARDEN

CONVERSATIONS WITH A SERIAL KILLER

ANNE K. HOWARD

http://wbp.bz/hisgardena

A lawyer gets inside the mind of a notorious New England serial killer in this award-winning and "grimly compelling" true crime (Kirkus).